Two Voices, One Story

Amy Masters
Elaine Rizzo

Published by Clink Street Publishing 2017

First edition.

ISBN: 978-1-911110-79-8 paperback
978-1-911110-80-4 ebook

To Tong Fang's birth mother and father, wherever you may be.

For Lee Masters, Amy's English Dad

and

For Wayne Rizzo, Amy's step-dad

who have both contributed to her upbringing.

Introduction (1)

My name is Amy Tong Fang Masters, and I am seventeen years old. I don't need to make up a story, to be honest, as my own life has been exciting enough for anyone.

You only have to look at my family to see that we are a bit unusual. I am Chinese, but my Mum is English, my step-dad is Maltese by origin and we live in Wales with two dogs and a couple of ferrets. My Mum and Dad are divorced, and most people think that my Dad must be Chinese, but he's English too, and lives in Birmingham. My step-mum is Chinese, though; but she's no real relation, other than by marrying my Dad.

So how can I be Chinese? Easy really – I was adopted as a baby from mainland China, and I have no idea who my Chinese mum and dad are.

The story is mine and my English Mum's – first our separate stories, then how we became mother and daughter, and finally what happened to us after that.

Some of the story is sad, some of it's funny, and some of it's nice. But all of it is true...

Introduction (2)

My name is Elaine Rizzo, also known as Elaine Masters, and I am Amy's "English" Mum. I am a bit older than seventeen years old, but I've always thought that the two things a woman should be secretive about are her age and her weight. So I'm not prepared to disclose either.

Adopting Amy WAS unquestionably the best thing I've ever done with my life. I've worried about her very often over the last seventeen years, but I don't think ninety plus per cent of my fussing has anything to do with her being from a different culture to me, or to her having been adopted. I think it's because mothers worry about their children. Full stop.

When Amy came to be adopted in 1999, there was a well-publicised one-child policy in China, which was relaxed two or three years ago in certain areas, but which has given rise to a generation of "missing" girls in that country. Our story is in no way a political one; it is the story of how one of those "missing" girls came to be adopted by a British couple and what happened afterwards, because the adoption itself was only the beginning in many ways.

In telling this story, I have deliberately left out very much detail concerning either my ex or my current husband. One of the reasons is because neither of them has a direct voice in the narrative, so all thoughts and feelings attributed to them would, therefore, be speculative. It is, however, mainly because we wanted the story to be predominately mine and Amy's, our very own "mother and daughter" drama.

I think Amy and I have both had fairly dramatic lives, if you compare us to a lot of other people. In fact, the very way we became mother and daughter was not without drama for each of us.

I strongly believe that it's not so much what happens to any of us in life that counts, but how we deal with it; this is what happened to both of us and how we dealt with it, individually and together.

I am also old enough to comprehend and appreciate Nietzsche's philosophy, which propounds the view "what doesn't kill me makes me strong."

Amy and I have each become a strong person. Or perhaps we are simply survivors...

Chapter One

In the Beginning

My story begins before Amy was even born.

Over the years I've learned to deal with being infertile, but it has taken me almost half my life to work through the various feelings and issues. I think what's finally left now is a factual rather than an emotive response to my condition.

My maternal grandmother's first child died as a baby, and the way she spoke about her deceased daughter was in a very matter-of-fact way. I didn't really understand this as a child; it took me years to realise the depth of feelings my Grandma must have worked through to be able to discuss her little girl in this way.

One reaction I've never been able to come to terms with completely, though, relates to the issue of femininity. I've never liked shopping, my interest in the house has always been sporadic at best, I've always worked in a profession which is almost entirely male dominated and the time I'm prepared to spent on clothes, hair and make-up is strictly limited. I've never been sure whether I really believe that I'm infertile because I'm unfeminine or whether I'm unfeminine because I'm infertile. Possibly each is a pre-requisite of the other.

Femininity is something which most women take for granted, but over which I have huge uncertainty with regards to myself. For years, I've studied others and found myself wondering what it's like to be a "real woman". I've never reached a definite conclusion over what this really means, only a hunch that it somehow doesn't apply to me.

My way to deal with this part of the story is to list the main facts for each of the most painful episodes.

In the far back year of 1995:

- I was married to a barrister who was attempting to establish his career.
- I had just passed my exams to qualify as a Licensed Insolvency Practitioner.
- I really enjoyed my job, and I was hoping to have a successful career.
- We jointly owned a four-bedroomed house, with two bathrooms, and a secluded garden, which we believed would be perfect for a family.
- I was then over thirty years old.
- I was the second child of a happily married, middle class couple and had been educated at a private girls' school.
- I came from a family where everyone was almost shockingly fertile (aunts, cousins, second cousins – my mother was one of eight children).
- No one else in my family, including my more remote family, was childless other than through their own choice at that time.
- I had never obtained any explanation over why I had apparently been unable to conceive for over the last six years.

- I had wasted at least the cost of one IVF treatment (without NHS funding) on ovulation predictor kits and pregnancy tests from various chemists and supermarkets.

- I was Auntie to three boys – two belonging to my elder sister, and one belonging to my **younger** brother.

- I managed to (almost) convince myself that between my nephews, my professional life, my marriage with our "social" life and holidays abroad, being childless did not much matter. I wouldn't allow it to.

- I no longer expected to become a parent.

And then, when I was least expecting it, the unthinkable actually happened and I actually was pregnant.

I really thought I had everything then – husband, career, home, family and a baby on the way. Does pride come before a fall? I don't know, but I do know this much: self-satisfaction most certainly does.

Because in 1995, I got pregnant and it changed my life, but not in a way that I could possibly ever have imagined.

Okay, so my Mum's right. I wasn't yet born when all this was going on.

BUT, she's not the only one who can list out difficult/painful facts.

In 1995, when my Mum was living in England, in mainland China:

- *There was a one-child policy in place, so it was almost impossible to bring up more than one child due to being fined for having more children. The fines were so large that most families just wouldn't have been able to pay them.*

- *Especially in the countryside, everyone wanted a boy. Because there were no state benefits in China, when you were old, you would be looked after by a son and his family.*

- *You would not live with a daughter, because she would have to help look after her husband's parents. So you might starve or have nowhere to live or no one to look after you if you were ill.*

- *Baby girls were left in various places, sometimes just to die.*

- *To abandon a child in China is a crime. The punishment is to go to prison.*

- *The children's homes in the countryside were full of girls, although there were some boys with disabilities.*

- *There was not much chance of surviving the conditions of the children's homes, as there was hardly any money to spend on the things babies need. They were also dark and cramped, although some of them didn't look so bad from the outside. You just wouldn't want to live there for very long.*

- *People from the West and sometimes from within China were allowed to adopt these girls, but there were loads of them for every one person or family wanting to do this. The chances of getting adopted from here were not all that high.*

- *At that time, babies living in the children's homes belonged to the state in China and they had no chance of having a loving home unless they were adopted.*

- *This means that there was no provision ever made for them to go to school, or to marry or to have their own child or even to earn any money. If they lived long enough.*

- *In any case, after a childhood living in an enclosed home, by the time that they became grown up, these babies had become institutionalised, resulting in all kinds of disabilities, including mental health issues.*

- *The homes had hardly any money, so the children had no toys, hardly any food, and often had to wear clothes that were almost in rags.*

- *You've only got to watch the documentary made in the same year my Mum is writing about (1995) once and you will never forget it. It's called "The Dying Rooms".*

So there I was, finally pregnant, after six years of "trying" (a terrible expression, if ever there was one, which conjures up quite a multitude of thoughts). My first reaction was one of shock and to tell the truth, it took me a few weeks to get used to the idea. I literally couldn't believe it at all to start with.

My GP confirmed the early stages of pregnancy, and arranged for me to see the practice mid-wife. After the first twelve weeks, we both told our families and work colleagues.

I had no morning sickness, and continued to commute to work every day, still doing the same fairly demanding job. My job consisted of working on liquidations, receiverships, bankruptcies, compositions with creditors – attempting to create some kind of order out of the financial chaos caused by others, absorbing some of their stress whilst trying to reach a workable solution and working to strict legal deadlines.

I don't remember all that much about being pregnant, apart from how numbingly tired I was all the time. I felt like I had been drained of all energy and I would sleep at the weekends for between twelve to fourteen hours at a time. Dreamless sleeps, drifting on and on like a dead man's float.

The first sign I had that anything might be wrong was when I began to feel ill. Whenever I ate anything, I began to feel really sick, but right in the pit of my stomach, like I had swallowed something poisonous.

The day it happened, when I was about sixteen weeks pregnant, I went to work, just as usual. I remember having stomach pains, only they were worse than usual, a dragging pain and feeling deathly tired. There was a diversion on the drive home and I remember missing my way completely and driving all over the place. Unusually for me, who has always considered myself as well able to deal with most things, I was deeply distressed and virtually in tears over this.

I remember getting home and saying to Lee, my ex-husband, that I didn't feel well and was going straight to bed. He brought my supper up on a tray; I must have fallen asleep after that. I don't remember him coming back into the room or even coming to bed.

I woke during the night, and the next part is seared on my brain for all time:

- Blood. Lots of it.
- Panic and fear. Even more of that.
- Getting an emergency appointment at the hospital and being too scared to think about it. (I later threw away the clothes that I was wearing when I visited the hospital.)
- Hospital staff and scanning machines. No one looking directly at me or meeting my eyes.
- Dead baby (male).
- The consultant asking me if I was scared of the operation I needed to get rid of his remains, in case I didn't wake up.
- Being scared I WOULD wake up afterwards and have to live with what had happened.
- Getting on a stretcher to have the operation.
- Waking up to a long night of sleeplessness, tears, more tears and overwhelming despair.

- And throughout this the knowledge of the tears and heart-break of my husband.

- We had conceived a child, who died in my womb, and after trying to self-abort, his remains were scraped from me and incinerated.

- Harsh, but no more nor less than the stark reality. Nothing can be gained from not facing up to reality, however unpleasant. And so I made myself face up to the unvarnished truth. I'm nothing if not a realist by nature.

Afterwards, I felt like nothing would ever be right in the world again, alternating with disbelief that this had really happened. I even thought that things like this didn't happen to me, that my life was too ordered for something like this.

Given my track record, I realised straight away that pregnancy was never going to happen to me again and that I had lost my chance forever to give birth to a child. (This turned out to be completely correct. I have a thin womb lining, and eggs are unable to "embed" there. we later paid privately to see a specialist consultant, but I found this completely distressing since he never seemed to give us any good news.)

I felt guilt as well as grief – that I must have done something to deserve this, or it wouldn't have happened. I began racking my brains to think what this could have been. Had I eaten or drank something which caused it? Had I stressed too much about work or been working too hard? Had there been signs that something was wrong and I had missed them? Could I have done anything differently and would it have changed the outcome?

Questions, questions going round and round in my mind to which there were no definitive answers and never would be. Well, not for me in this life, anyway.

All in all these were very dark days, whilst I struggled to come to terms with my grief and the massive loss of the only child I would ever conceive.

I would like to say that this all brought me closer to Lee, that we shared our sense of loss. In truth, it only brought us closer in part. I think one of the worst aspects of great grief is its isolating nature. Something we each have to seek to come to terms with on our own and in our own way.

The other terrible aspect of grief is, of course, the fear it engenders. That cruel smack in the face, which is the reminder that anything can happen to anybody, at any time. And sometimes does.

Of course I went back to work, but I never talked about what had happened. I was a very private person in those days, but the loss of my child was so intense that I now wonder how I managed to function. I only know that there is still a tiny, fragile core of me that nobody will be able share with me over this. Ever.

I still remember my child on the anniversary of my miscarriage, but I am well aware that it is a date no one but me ever remembers. Why would they? My son never existed outside of my body, so who but his mother would ever remember the exact date of the day/night he died? Or ever think of the day he should have been born?

I used to look at photographs in the newspaper reporting the abuse or neglect of a little child and I would stroke his or her face, thinking, "I wouldn't have done that to you." Of course it wasn't fair on anybody whichever way you looked at it, but whoever guaranteed or even claimed that life was fair? It's just that it sometimes feels very hard when you're the one on the receiving end of its unfairness.

I later met other women who were unable to have children and who told me that they too used to do this or something similar, so it must be a more common reaction than I realised at the time.

If grief is isolating, then so too is childlessness, however much I had tried put a brave face on things over the years. It's also a very taboo subject.

Over time, the colour of my grief over the loss of my son and over my inability to give birth to a child has changed, starting off red and angry, through black and grey despair, then over the years finally turning from blue to green to yellow. These days, the colour of my grief is gold, which is something that I can live with.

When I first sought help, though, it was the raw colours of red and black.

For those who have never experienced the condition of infertility :

- It is very hard to stand by and watch other people start and finish families in the time it has taken you to get precisely nowhere, even though you feel that you have already run the race several times over.

- Almost everyone who has children takes them for granted for lots of the time, even when they love them deeply.

- When you have children, I'm sure it must be difficult to imagine a situation where you will never hold a child from your own body in your arms, however much you might want to.

- The need to reproduce is a simple and almost animal instinct, which doesn't require deep thought. That only happens when the capacity to do this is denied.

- The desire to leave behind a permanent "thumbprint" on the world before it is too late, not to just lift out of life leaving nothing to show for ever having existed in the world, is stronger than any hunger or thirst or sex urge.

- For most of us, that desire is fulfilled by having children, which is our legacy to the future and our part in the much bigger cycle of life, with the prospect of the continuity of succeeding generations ahead of us. Our own little bit of immortality. It is, quite simply, part of being human or more specifically, part of being alive, since procreation is also a driving force in the animal kingdom.

- When you want children, but are denied having them, you are forced to examine some huge, huge issues, which might otherwise never occur to you.

- And I have to confess that I never did manage to come entirely to terms with some of these issues.

- I also have to report that I used to wake up every night having panic attacks that I would end up being childless. I could feel time ticking on and I was getting older. The deadly knowledge that I would never/could never give birth to a child felt like such a huge weight on top of me that I could hardly breathe. I would wake up filled with panic and fear.

- I would be the first to admit that some aspects of my behaviour were completely irrational in those days. For instance, I refused to shop in certain supermarkets at certain times, because everywhere I looked there seemed to be women with babies or couples with young families and seeing them just hurt too much.

- And absolutely everywhere I went, there were pregnant women. Or perhaps I just noticed them more than I used to.

I also took a dislike to the house which we'd bought a few years before, the one we'd intended to have as our own "family" home. So I insisted that we sold it and moved to a smaller one in a nearby village where we had friends and where my sister lived with her two boys.

Looking back down the years now, I really believe that at this stage in my life, I was in danger of getting locked in my own misery, bitterness and helpless despair over what had happened, especially as I just couldn't see any way out of it.

I don't know what would have happened if Alexander (Mum's son she lost) hadn't died before he was born.

Maybe I would have had an older brother. But Mum says not.

So maybe I would never have been adopted at all. I would probably have just been left in a children's home and then I don't have a clue what would have happened to me once I got too old to live there.

I might have been adopted by someone else. Someone really, really rich with their own horses and swimming pool would have been pretty cool. But then it might have been by someone horrid and unkind. So I think I'm better off with Mum, who really loves me and I know she would do practically anything for me.

She says it was part of her destiny – and our joint destiny – for her baby to have died. She's explained to me that this is part of how she came to adopt me.

I've asked her a few times what she thinks he would have been like if he was alive. My Mum says that it took her years to realise it, but no one is allowed to know what would have happened in life. We can only know what has happened and what is happening now.

She also says that she thinks it's a funny question and that she doesn't know what he would have been like as she never thinks about that herself, because it was something that just didn't happen.

I don't think it's a funny question, though. I think it's only natural to think about people who are part of you and what they might have been like or the things they might have done or said.

I sometimes think about my Chinese family. But I particularly think about my Chinese mum and what she might have been like and how she would look now.

Fortunately for me, I didn't get totally lost inside my own grief or bitterness in the end. A few things happened to prevent me from doing this.

The first one seems like only a small thing, but actually had a HUGE impact on me.

I was lying in bed early one morning trying to persuade myself to get up and face the world, after one of those nights – sleepless, teeth chattering round a tea cup clutched for comfort, when there seemed to be no possible comfort. My husband had Radio 4 on listening to the news, when "Thought for the Day" came on.

A middle aged clergyman was talking about children and young people. He was explaining how hard it was for some children in the care system, who had to face up to difficult issues and how some of them had no family there to help them to deal with it, or to be there for them in the long term. That they had to deal with some of the realities of life on their own or, at best, with paid help and that there were children all over the world who were unwanted.

People sometimes say that they hear "a call" from God and become converted to Christianity. That didn't happen to me, but I did feel very humbled whilst listening to that broadcast. I was in my thirties before I really had to face up to anything terrible and, however much some things had to be faced up to by myself, I did have a family. I knew how I felt and could only begin to imagine what it must be like to be a child, scared and alone.

The second help came when I voluntarily started to see a therapist for hypno- and psycho-therapy sessions. For the first time, I was able to talk through all my fears and concerns over pregnancy and childlessness without feeling I was distressing or burdening anyone else.

The first session I had was one of hypno-therapy because I was so deeply wounded by what had happened that I was completely unable to talk about how I felt, which is very unusual for me, as I have always had plenty to say. Contrary to my previous ideas about being hypnotised, I was conscious the whole time and I could remember everything that I said; its effect was to allow me to express the thoughts and feelings from my subconscious which I had previously not wanted to face up to.

Initially, this was very distressing, because I was forced to reveal thoughts and feelings which I had buried deeply inside myself over the months, but after a few sessions, I started to feel able to face up to some of them.

In one of the later sessions I described my fear of pregnancy, describing the blood and black despair of it all, which I described as a massive wall right in front of me, which I couldn't seem to get past or around or over the top of, because I knew there was no happy outcome for me. I mentioned that I would like to go for adoption, but that I thought this would be "cheating".

When I was asked why I thought this, I said because it felt like I would be "sneaking below the wall and avoiding all the pain to get on the other side". My therapist asked me why this was such a bad thing and why I needed to put myself through unnecessary suffering. I had to admit that I didn't know and probably just thought that I should. It actually didn't make much sense when you put it like that.

I feel that I should write this in very small letters – I will always be ashamed that during all my years of infertility, I never thought of adopting a child. It wasn't until I experienced my own personal tragedy and found out for myself how bleak life can sometimes be, that this even occurred to me. More shame on me.

Lee and I then went to a conference on infertility, where I picked up an out of date magazine that someone had meant to throw away. When I got home, I read a letter on Overseas Adoption from a woman who ran a voluntary support agency called OASIS, which helped couples to adopt from a few countries all over the world.

I wrote away for some information and I wondered if I dared to do this. I rang the woman at her home in the Welsh valleys, to find that she had adopted two children from Thailand over a decade before.

For the first time, someone really seemed to understand how I felt; it was as though, from miles away, she put a metaphorical arm around my shoulders in complete solidarity. She also made me believe that I really did have the courage to go ahead and to try to adopt a child from overseas.

The information we received was for adoption from various countries, but particularly from China, with its one-child policy. There were literally thousands of baby girls, barely surviving in the most horrendous conditions imaginable.

And so began our twenty-month-long application to be allowed to adopt our daughter.

The worst North China flood in forty years happened in the spring of 1998, when there was massive flooding of parts of the Yangtze River.

Seemingly:

- *Over 4,000 people were lost.*
- *Over 25 million acres were evacuated.*
- *15 million people were made homeless.*
- *180 million people were affected by it.*

So, you see, I wasn't the only one to have her life changed by this particular act of nature.

And I really don't remember it because I was just a tiny baby of not even a few months old.

But it did shape the entire course of my life, if that is what is meant by "affected".

The adoption process itself was actually fairly interesting, once I had learned to take a big step back from it and to view it as a unique experience in itself.

For me, this was the best way of dealing with what seemed like a lengthy and bureaucratic process when we first began it. I still think for anyone contemplating the adoption process, it would be better to consider and to deal with each stage at a time, rather than trying to look at the whole all at once to prevent it from seeming endless or daunting.

We initially had to be interviewed by the head of Social Services from our local authority to assess our basic suitability. She seemed to be inclining us towards local adoption of older children. It was difficult to determine whether this was some kind of "test" – if we insisted on considering overseas adoption only, would we be considered too narrow-minded and inflexible? But if we said we would consider this, would this suggest lack of commitment to overseas adoption?

I did suggest that we might ultimately like to consider both, but I was pretty smartly advised that if we went for overseas adoption, we would be considered to be a "mixed race" family, which would exclude us from domestic adoption. It was clearly an "either/or" situation then, without very much time to think.

We were also told that if we chose the option of adopting from overseas that once the process was over, we would be entirely on our own and that the local Social Services department would not provide us with any help or support, including during the time when our child first returned home to live with us.

In the end, we opted to ask if we could discuss it overnight and telephone with our decision the next day, which we did, electing to go for overseas adoption.

We decided on this for two reasons, really. Firstly, that as neither of us had ever been parents before, we believed that we needed to develop as parents as our child was developing – therefore, with a very young child or a baby. Secondly, no child in the UK dies as a direct result of not being adopted (possibly, and sadly, as a result of the authorities not intervening soon enough, but that's a whole other issue), which was clearly not the case in China.

Because we had elected to go for overseas adoption, we had to pay for an independent social worker to assess whether we were suitable to adopt. We were extremely lucky here, as Rob, the social worker we were allocated, was easy to talk to and very helpful over the potential issues we might encounter if our application was to prove successful.

In fact, we began the first session by stating that we couldn't believe that the purpose of the assessment was to "trick us" or catch us out in any way, but was rather to help us to establish whether we were suitable and whether we had considered all aspects of the adoption fully. We added that we hoped he would assist us with some ideas of his own over how to deal with some of the challenges facing us.

How could he disagree? And it led to some interesting and stimulating discussions over the future welfare of our daughter.

In one of our discussions, we all determined that if we had met in other circumstances, we might all have ended up becoming friends and he even apologised to us for having to search our house on random visits. Of course we understood that this was part of the assessment function.

We also understood when he cancelled appointments with us at the last minute for emergencies which had arisen; however impatient I was, I could imagine that the issues which Rob was dealing with on some occasions were way more critical than a further visit to see us.

I will say, as an observation, though, that I consider the adoption process was weighted, at least at that time, in favour of middle-class applicants, if for no other reason than that we were more used to dealing with "authority". This was a shame, as it probably put off some potentially very good parents and I did later report this to our local MP with some ideas over how the process could be re-appraised in this respect.

I will also say that initially when dealing with Social Services, we felt we had to play down any material advantages that we would be able to offer our daughter; this contrasted strongly with the attitude of the communist Chinese authorities when we were over there, who seemed to take the view that you couldn't offer too many of these.

In addition, both Lee and I had to have health checks which were carried out by our local GP and police checks to establish that neither of us had a criminal record.

In any case, our application was approved by our local authority in due course and all our papers were forwarded by the Department of Health to the China Center of Adoption Affairs (CCAA). We were assured that now we need only wait.

Chapter Two

China Girl

I was born near Tongling, in Anhui Province, mainland China, which is on the southern banks of the Yangtze River, in mid-April 1998.

Tongling is a copper producing region, with many of the people outside of the small city living from what they could grow on the land. Anhui Province was one of the poorest regions in China at the end of the twentieth century. It has a mild climate, but also has lots of rain.

My birth date was told to my English Mum and Dad as 15 April, but I don't think anyone really knows the exact date. All they know is that I was left at the gates of the Tong Ling Welfare Centre where I was found on 30 May 1998 and that the welfare centre's advisory doctor thought I was about six weeks old at the time.

I don't know who left me there or why. I know that the time this happened was when the Yangtze had flooded the area. The effects of the flooding on the area around Tongling must have been more terrible that I can even imagine. Years later, as a teenager, when I went to a spiritual meeting a psychic who was there told me she thought I must've been born in a war zone, due to the fear, despair and devastation she could sense surrounding my place of birth.

I also know that whoever left me wanted me to be found and cared for, because of where I was left. And that whoever it was took a big risk over getting caught and punished.

Obviously, I don't remember anything about this. Whenever I imagine what happened, I always think of my Chinese mum, waiting until it was dark, and plucking up the courage to take me there.

I think of her with long black hair – a lot like mine is now – and being young, alone, and very afraid. I see her holding me close and then looking all round until the coast was clear. I imagine her placing me carefully at the gates and then running away fast, without looking back and with tears streaming down her cheeks which fall on the floor as she runs.

Always it is my Chinese mum I think of leaving me there, never my dad or any other member of my family. I don't know why I think this though. Maybe it's because I think it was most likely to have been her.

Of course, it might not have been like that all. That's just what I imagine it was like.

I was found and taken into the welfare centre to be looked after; as well as choosing my birthday for me, the staff there also gave me my Chinese name, which is Tong Fang. This means "Copper Child."

It seemed like the waiting to hear from the Chinese authorities would never end.

In fact, the whole process from when we first contacted our local social services to the date of our arrival in China took twenty months in total. There was a period of about six months of complete inactivity when all our papers had gone off to the authorities in China and there was literally nothing we could do to hurry things on.

We used to play a waiting game of "well say they got our application by such and such a date. And then they put it at the back of the pile, which takes six months to get to the bottom of. Then take off a one-month delay in China for the Chinese New Year at the end of January to end of February, then they write to the Department of Health, who wait a few weeks to write us, this means we should hear something by blah date."

I was beginning to fear that our application had got lost somewhere along the way, when Lee rang me on 13 April 1999 at about 8.00 am. I had left the house early for a meeting and just as he was due to leave himself, a courier had arrived with papers containing a tiny photograph, with the medical details, written in Chinese of a small child, Tong Fang, currently living in a welfare centre in a far-away district in China.

I went straight home, called in the office and took the rest of the day off. To say I was slightly unnerved is something of an understatement.

Lee took the details of our future daughter to the Chinese medical centre in Chinatown, Birmingham, who provided us with a translation. So far as we could determine, Tong Fang seemed to be in good health.

We were so intrigued by the passport sized snap of Tong Fang. We learned that her birthday was 15 April 1998, so she was about to have her first birthday. The photograph had been taken of her on Christmas Day 1998, when she was taken to a medical centre for injections to "prepare" her for her adoption.

Although my daughter was alone on her very first Christmas – a time of family and of sharing – I was glad to know that at least her day had been spent in completing formalities in the anticipation of eventually meeting her new family.

We never found out what selection method was used for Tong Fang to be placed with us; we will never know whether there was a scientific basis for this or whether it was a pure random act on the part of the Chinese authorities. I have always believed that the method was unimportant and that Tong Fang was destined to be my daughter, just as I was destined to be her mother for the rest of our respective lives.

Over the next few weeks, we used to study the tiny small photograph of her in great detail, imagining that we could detect character traits from looking at it. All nonsense, of course, but my initial assessment of "she looks self-willed" has turned out to be one hundred per cent correct.

After the recent months of inactivity, the time was suddenly here. The next weeks were taken up by organizing our travel arrangements. We both received a letter of invitation to travel to China, to obtain our visas from the Chinese Embassy so that we could book our journey to meet our daughter.

In 1999, China had only just begun to open its doors to the Western world, so the arrangements for entry were even stricter than they are today.

The travel company also had to arrange for us to have a translator/ guide in both Anhui Province and later on in Beijing, where we would have to travel with our daughter to complete the adoption formalities.

We were to meet our daughter in Hefei, which is the capital city of Anhui, approximately eight weeks after we first received the details of our little Tong Fang.

Although we knew that our daughter had just had her first birthday, we actually had no idea of what size she would be, as we had heard reports from other members of the support group who had successfully adopted that their own daughters had been smaller than the clothes they had brought from the UK for the age group.

We were advised to take baby clothes for a variety of ages, from ages six to eighteen months old, particularly as it was usual to leave anything which didn't fit with the staff from the welfare centre for use by the other babies living in their care.

We were also advised to take disposable nappies, blankets, bottles, formula milk, some jars of baby food, baby cosmetics, including creams and a few small toys. So we bought a massive hold all bag and packed it full of baby things.

We packed a smaller suitcase with our own clothes for a two-week stay.

Then we booked the local taxi company in our Midlands village to take us to Heathrow Airport and so on Saturday 5 June 1999, we finally left home to catch the night flight to Beijing to find our tiny daughter.

Naturally, I don't remember what was happening to me whilst my English parents were getting ready to come to China.

My Mum said afterwards that she was panicking about whether they'd got everything they needed and whether they would meet up with the guide to start with and then with me. She said they were also worried about whether I would be ill or whether I would even like with her and my English Dad.

Several years later, my Mum, my Dad and I used to play a game (which I really liked) called "Amy is adopted by her loving parents."

During the part where my Mum and Dad were pretending that they were on the aeroplane, I used to lie on a cushion sometimes pretending to gurgle to myself and sometimes pretending to be asleep, but I was really listening to them talking about how excited and nervous they both were.

We carried on playing this game until I got too big to be picked up and put in my Mum's arms.

I wasn't excited or nervous that I can remember, because I was just too little to have any idea what was going on.

I would be lying if I didn't admit that I was feeling incredibly nervous as well as excited once we began our journey; there was so much at stake here, including the future welfare and happiness of Tong Fang.

During the Saturday eleven-hour evening/night flight to Beijing, I managed to sleep only intermittently in between watching feature-length movies and being offered refreshments by the air steward and stewardess. My mind was chasing round full of thoughts. Would our daughter be healthy? Would she bond with us? Would our being from a different culture be an insuperable obstacle? Would she be happy living with us?

Incidentally, our stewardess was young (about twenty five years old), Chinese by origin and it is only fair to say that both Lee and I agreed that we had rarely seen such a beautiful and lively girl. Of course, this gave rise to further speculation about what Tong Fang herself might eventually grow up to be like.

So the long night passed and we arrived at Beijing Airport on Sunday 6 June 1999 feeling tired, nervous and dishevelled. In fact, when I went to the cloakroom for a wash and clean up, I distinctly remember looking at myself in the mirror and wondering what I was doing there, miles from home, trying to adopt a child who might not even want anything to do with me.

I'd seen flights to Hong Kong on the departure board and in a mad moment, I contemplated checking in on a flight to there, having a holiday and then returning home, pretending I'd never even heard of overseas adoption. Yes, I was having a type of panic attack.

But I realised that as soon as we'd boarded the mythical flight to Hong Kong, I would immediately regret it bitterly for the rest of my life. By the time I'd wiped my eyes, given my nose a good blow and washed my face, my resolve was back and I left the cloakroom, feeling rather foolish.

When I confessed to Lee what had happened, he admitted that when we were on the flight between London and Beijing, he'd had a compulsion to open the emergency exit and to just jump out into the night, in an act of panic. He said it had felt like a perfectly reasonable thing to have done at the time.

We laughed at each other and ourselves, agreeing that we had each been prey to feeling overwrought, being full of perfectly natural nervous apprehension coupled with the tiredness and excitement of the journey. Feeling so much better, we began to look around us a little at the busy airport to make the most of our experience or our "great adventure", as I insisted on terming it.

Although it was Sunday, the airport was teeming with people. My first impression was of just how many people there were around. And just how very many people there were around. Considering that I had lived and worked in three UK cities – Manchester, London and Birmingham – I was immediately struck by the sheer volume of people. I began to have some comprehension over why China had adopted a one-child policy, even if I could never have any empathy with its consequences to baby girls.

We had to find our internal flight to Hefei, where we were to be met by our guide/translator. This was another source of concern to me, now we were so close. Would he or she come to meet us? Would they know what arrangements had been made for us to be united with our daughter? What if something had gone wrong and Tong Fang's welfare centre were not expecting us?

The only thing to do, of course, was to find the flight to Hefei and to find out what was what when we got there. We found the gate number for our flight, noticing that we were the only Westerners.

I initially felt greatly disadvantaged by being in a country where I could not speak or understand the language and was completely unfamiliar with its customs. As our adventure unfolded, however, we met with such courtesy and genuine help that this proved to be no real barrier to communication at all.

Almost immediately, we had a most heart warming experience, where kind and delicate courtesy was extended to two foreign travellers far from home. Whilst waiting for the flight to Hefei, Lee and I had both settled into two extremely comfortable easy chairs and had nodded off to sleep after our troubled night. The flight to Hefei was called, but we slept through it.

We were each awakened by a gentle tap on the shoulder from a small boy, aged about five years old, who we had noticed earlier with the family sitting opposite us. We both awoke to find the family nodding and smiling at us and both of us were so much less startled than if we'd been woken up by a grown up.

We hurried to board our internal flight to Hefei feeling profoundly relieved and grateful.

During the flight, the refreshments offered were in a pre-packed box, containing chopsticks, dried seaweed and a spring roll with a cup of fragrant Chinese tea.

Although we were the only Westerners on the flight, the head stewardess, after making her normal take off speech in Chinese, made a special speech just for us in English, welcoming us on board. The same happened when we landed; we were thanked for travelling and bid farewell to.

It is true that some of her English was a little jumbled, but the sentiments were very clear and were much appreciated by us, who were completely ignorant ourselves in the Chinese language. It was a wonderful gesture of acknowledgement on her part and on behalf of the rest of the crew.

Once we had collected our luggage, we were met by our guide (so much for my previous unfounded worries in this respect) who told us that her Western name was Lisa. She was a twenty three year-old student, studying architecture at the university, who acted as a guide and did translation work to support herself in her studies.

We were clearly exhausted from travelling and Lisa advised us to get a good night's sleep, because it had been arranged that in the morning Tong Fang would be brought to our hotel so we could complete the adoption formalities.

What thoughts and feelings were coursing through me on that last night of involuntary childlessness? Feelings of excitement, trepidation, disbelief and a sense of unreality that the time had finally arrived were uppermost in my mind.

My biggest fears were over Tong Fang's health and over whether she would bond with me or ever accept me as her "mother".

The tiny picture we had of our daughter which had been taken on Christmas Day and sent to us with the adoption papers had already been pored over many times and we were unable to resist scanning every little detail of it over again on the evening we arrived in China.

In our restlessness, we decided to take a stroll around the city in the early evening. We were away from the cities where Westerners commonly travelled for business or pleasure. It is, therefore, unsurprising that we attracted attention or that residents we encountered turned to stare openly at us. We quickly realised none of the attention directed towards us was hostile; it was sheer curiosity and wonder as in those days, many of the local people had probably not seen many Westerners in person before, if any at all.

I'd like to say that I took Lisa's advice, but I had a very disturbed night's sleep, dozing off fitfully, before awaking very early in the morning, knowing that further sleep was impossible.

We had an early breakfast, as I've always found a cup of hot, sweet tea steadies my nerves (oh, but how very English that makes me sound). The buffet breakfast room was filled with other Western couples, who had all travelled from Canada to adopt daughters, many of whom seemed to know one another although I have to comment that most of them looked as nervous as I was feeling.

We met Lisa in the hotel at the time she had appointed the previous night, to be informed that Tong Fang, the assistant director of the welfare centre and one of the nannies had been delayed on the journey from Tong Ling.

Afraid to go very far, we ordered a large pot of tea and another of coffee for us all to share, whilst we sat and waited an unspecified time for our daughter. After all, having waited so long and travelled so far, what difference did a further slight delay make, except possibly to our nerves?

I have always been amazed how, with so many million inhabitants in China, the authorities arranged to get one tiny child to a foreign couple on a specifically appointed day at a specifically appointed time.

But so it was, because no sooner had we poured our tea/coffee than Lisa jumped up and said, "Here's your baby arriving now!"

I too jumped up and saw a lovely baby with a mass of black hair being carried into the reception by a young girl who was accompanied by an older woman.

I could tell straight away that it was Tong Fang by her eyes. We had planned to take a photograph of our daughter arriving, but due to the unexpected timing, we missed that exact second.

But no matter – our baby daughter was here at last and this was my over-riding thought as I took her into my arms for the first time. And I have to confess that I did shed a few tears of joy.

I've still got the clothes that I arrived in – a tiny pair of stretch dungarees which are for a baby of six months old (although I was about fourteen months old at the time), a frayed, old top, a pair of very thin socks and some scuffed shoes, with laces which were tied round my ankles to keep them on.

Photographs show that I had a thick head of short, black hair and I think that I look quite pretty.

I couldn't sit up properly or anything, but there are pictures of me propped up against pillows or cushions so that I could look round.

My English parents brought new clothes over for me, as well as soft blankets, and a few small toys.

On the first day, I chose a Teletubby toy and I spent a while (so I'm told) choosing between Po (the smallest and red one) and Lala (the next smallest and yellow) before eventually cuddling up to Po.

It seems that I liked formula milk, but when my Mum put a small piece of rusk on my tongue, I just wiped it straight off again.

It was my Dad who gave me my first bottle and then he and my Mum took more photos of me with them, the assistant director of the welfare centre and the young nanny.

After a short while, my carers from the welfare centre left me with my new Mum and Dad and with Lisa, our translator; they waved goodbye in the foyer of the hotel and I never saw them again.

Once we had Tong Fang safely in our arms, figuratively and literally, there were still lots of formalities to complete.

We had to complete adoption papers, which we were all required to sign. As our daughter was so tiny, she had to have her foot inked up, so as to leave her foot print on the documents as a mark of her own consent to the process.

Amy Tong Fang's official adoption date was 7 June 1999.

We showed the clothes we had brought with us from the UK to Lisa and the ladies from the welfare centre, holding them up against Tong Fang.

As we had brought a whole range of sizes with us, not all of them fitted her. All were simple things – baby-grows, little jumpers and dresses all from high street stores. I particularly remember a very lovely little striped, lightweight anorak, which had not been very expensive, but was cute and weather proof for the spring and summer months, which did not fit our daughter.

We offered all the clothes which did not immediately fit Tong Fang to the welfare centre for the use of other children in their care. Both ladies were so touchingly pleased and grateful for our gift that I've always, ever afterwards, said that this is one of the most humbling experiences of my life.

We were in a country where survival itself was no guarantee and not everyone had access at that time to some of the simplest things that we all take for granted in the Western world.

Once we had said goodbye, with many thanks and some personal gifts to the ladies from the welfare centre to thank them for looking after our daughter, we had to complete a further part of the adoption formalities by going before the governor for whom we had brought a gift of whiskey and cigarettes. It was at this point that we had to select our daughter's English name for her.

Based on the photograph, we had decided to name her "Amy" because we thought it suited her; it means "well-loved". Amy's Chinese name was retained as her middle names, so from that time, tiny Tong Fang has been known on a daily basis by her Western name of Amy.

Lee and I both had to agree that we would care for daughter's welfare for the rest of our lives (which promise, I believe, we have both completely honoured to the present date) and there were quite a number of documents for us to sign before the authorities. Amy herself had to appear with us for the formalities, but being a baby, she was obviously too young to take part in or to understand any of the formalities.

It was here that we were questioned fully and frankly by the governor about our income, our home and our family backgrounds, including what financial advantages we were able to offer our child.

We also obtained a Chinese passport for our daughter, so that she would be able to travel back to the UK with us. We were already aware that once we had all the Chinese adoption papers, we wouldn't need to re-adopt Amy for us to be her legal parents in Britain, due to the conventions over child adoption which had been ratified in both countries.

Once the local adoption formalities were complete, we bathed Amy in the sink of our hotel bathroom and changed her as her bottom and upper legs were covered in sores because she had never before worn a nappy. We also washed and conditioned her thick head of hair, which was initially rather coarse in texture, but which soon began to look and feel like silk.

Thank goodness for baby creams and lotions, soaps and shampoos – poor Amy spent the first few days being washed and covered in different creams for her face, her hands plus her limbs and her nether regions.

We dressed her in a new little baby-grow we had bought with us, which made her look even prettier; I've still kept this first little outfit along with other things from our journey to China.

We were then looking forward to getting to know our beautiful daughter and spending some time together as a family.

I can't believe that my Mum nearly killed me on my very first day with her!

The assistant director of the welfare centre had told my parents that I liked eggs and apple juice, so my Mum and Dad went to a restaurant in the hotel and ordered scrambled eggs for me. My Mum put a small amount of scrambled egg in my mouth which caused me to start choking.

My Dad had to pat my back and pull the piece of egg out of my mouth.

My Mum grabbed me up, took me to our room, leaving her own lunch, so she could make me some formula milk and feed me apricot and rice puree from a jar, as suitable for small babies, which she had brought with her.

She always says this began her obsession over who is eating what and when and how much, so even to this day she is always trying to force food on my friends and keeps our house well-stocked with food, as it was obvious that I had been given very limited food to this point.

She says she was worried that I would never overcome these deficiencies unless she fed me nutritionally.

I wouldn't drink apple juice for years either – I just used to spit it out – so I wonder which baby the assistant director was talking about as it seems that there were a lot of us under her care, so she probably got confused between me and one of the many other babies in the welfare centre's care.

The very first night that we put Amy into her cot in the hotel room, although still tired from the journey and the previous night's lack of sleep, I hardly slept as I could sense that she was awake in her cot.

I tried walking round with her and pushing her round in her push-chair to see if I could get her to drop off to sleep, but without any success.

She must have been completely terrified to have been taken from the only place she knew – whatever the conditions of the welfare centre might have been – and to have been thrust into the arms of complete strangers, who didn't even look or sound like anyone she'd ever seen before.

She didn't cry and I immediately realised that she had gotten to the stage of not crying because nobody would come if she did.

It still tears me apart to remember how she used to silently comfort herself by nuzzling and sucking at the top of the inside of her own arm whenever she was distressed.

I can hardly write this even now as the sense of the fear, isolation and deep despair which my daughter must have experienced as a tiny baby, and the knowledge that she could have had no other comfort that to turn to her own self in this way, still deeply distresses me whenever I recall that tiny image of her.

I can only say that for a considerable time, whenever Amy didn't sleep, neither did I and there was a time in my life – which many new mothers will empathise with – when I managed to function with very little sleep.

It was clear the next day that there was something wrong with Amy because she was so fretful and wouldn't settle or eat at all and she had a hacking cough and her breathing was rather laboured.

We spoke to Lisa, our interpreter, who looked at our daughter and suggested that we take her to Hefei hospital, where a paediatric doctor had to be summoned in especially, as it was a Sunday.

We went by taxi and whilst I was preoccupied in soothing Amy, Lee was terrified by the reckless driving as we literally screeched to the hospital.

Amy was diagnosed as suffering from bronchitis and prescribed a course of painkillers and antibiotics which soon took effect and she was cured within a very few days. We were greatly relieved and very grateful to the doctor who was so willing to have her Sunday interrupted to help strangers who, in our case, were also foreigners.

It is strange to think that I was so ill on my first day with my English parents that I had to be dashed to the hospital and given medication.

All through school and even as a teenager, I am almost never ill – I think I've only ever had about one sick day off school or college each academic year.

Between my Mum nearly choking me and then me being handed over to them with bronchitis, plus the taxi driving like a bat out of hell, it seems I had a very dramatic time during my first forty eight hours with my new parents.

I was given a small rattle in the shape of a strawberry which had a smiley face on it by one of the waitresses at the hotel, when I got back from the hospital.

My Dad rigged up a paper chain for me so that he could swing "Mr Strawberry" from one side of my cot towards me, where I was propped up on the other side, making the little bell inside my new toy ring as it swung forwards.

It seems that I was absolutely delighted by this, finding the performance so very funny that I laughed really hard every time my Dad swung Mr Strawberry towards me.

It was the first time my parents had heard me laugh out loud and it was also one of the first sounds I had ever made in front of them.

Once Amy was restored to health, the next few days in Hefei passed happily as we strolled around the city, looking at places of interest and just enjoying being together.

Hefei itself is a small city, which was roughly about the same size as the city of Derby in the UK, although with a more dense population.

There was beginning to be some evidence of Western influence in Hefei in 1999, although it seemed to have been fairly recent and in the main area of the city. For example, the hotel where we were staying was the main one in the city, which was a newly-built Holiday Inn, with several restaurants which served Chinese and American style food. There was also a shopping centre which sold a variety of consumer goods, including some well-known European brand names, but there was none of the fast food places which were springing up in the major cities in China at the end of the twentieth century.

Lisa acted as a guide to show us around places of historical interest which allowed Lee the opportunity to ask plenty of questions as he had done lots of reading over the years on Chinese history. I have to confess that I busied myself with looking after my baby during these exchanges.

We were asked by several groups of students from the university if we would agree to have our photographs taken for an exhibition, which we agreed to do, so somewhere in China there are photographs of us all relaxing on a sunny day – the East meets the West, so to speak.

We then had to travel Beijing to obtain an indefinite entry visa from the British embassy for Amy's entry into the UK.

While we were at the airport in Hefei waiting for our flight to Beijing, I was approached by an elderly Chinese lady (who looked like a grandma). She insisted on wrapping one of the blankets I'd brought round Amy, despite the heat (it was a hot day in June). We had found, by the way, that the Chinese were fanatical about wrapping babies up warmly in those days, even in the heat.

She then pointed to the sores, like little insect bites, which were on Amy's hands and legs, before launching into a very loud tirade against me, causing most of the other waiting passengers to stare over at us. Although my chastisement was all spoken in Chinese, I was left in little doubt of its content and I considered myself well and truly reprimanded.

I had absolutely no way of communicating with this matriarch to explain that I had only been my daughter's mother for a few days, that her condition was none of my doing and that, in fact, it was improving under my careful ointment of various creams, care, love and attention.

To say that Lee and I were stupefied with astonishment over the unprecedented attack is an understatement. The incident still causes Lee some amusement, as he tells Amy that this the only time anyone has ever been able to criticise her Mum for being a bad parent, particularly as the telling off was as unexpected as it was undeserved.

Before we left Anhui, Amy was presented with a copper medal, produced from the region of her birth, and stamped with an image of the bridge at Hefei, so that she will know that wherever she goes in her life and whatever she decides to do, she will always be a child of Anhui Province.

During our visit to Beijing to complete the adoption formalities, we also made a trip to Tiananmen Square, although we had to be accompanied on the visit there by Norman, our guide/translator in Beijing.

The statue of Chairman Mao dominates the centre of the square, together with statues of other famous Chinese revolutionaries, who are styled the People's Heroes. There were many visitors from all nationalities visiting there, all with guides, who were explaining the history to the different groups, generally, I noted, in English.

A very old lady who was clearing tables in one of the cafes was desperate to speak to me. Our guide said that she was trying to tell me that Amy was destined to be my daughter, something I have always believed myself. She also said that Amy is a lucky person as denoted by the shape of her earlobes and that she is beautiful because she has pale skin. Of course, as her Mother, I like to think that both of those things are true too.

We also visited Monument Square, which, in June 1999, had just been constructed in time for the Millennium celebrations, where we were shown the eternal flame. It would be lit at midnight on 1 January 2000, to symbolise the continuity of over five thousand years of the survival of the Chinese people, each person representing just a tiny dot in the whole history of China – without any one of whom the whole could not be complete.

It was moving and awe-inspiring to reflect that I too was now one of those very tiny dots in China's history of survival.

Once we had completed the rest of the adoption formalities, we had a few days of leisure to look around Beijing, which was quite literally teeming with people and traffic. I was also struck by the number of bicycles in the city, which seemed an extremely popular way of getting around; there were rows and rows of them parked along the paths on what seemed a continual basis.

The weather was warm and it was fun to stroll along; unlike Hefei, there were plenty of places to eat, from the traditional Chinese street cafes to the Western fast food places, with most things in between.

We couldn't fail to notice that there was a lot of construction around the city, which was taking place in preparation for Beijing's bid to host the 2008 Olympics (which seemed a far off date to us, as we looked round the city then).

We also didn't attract any particular attention simply because we were Westerners, although I did ask Norman whether there was any adverse feeling towards Westerners who adopted Chinese children. He told me that there wasn't, because most Chinese people realised that this was the child's only way of finding a permanent home and that it meant continuity of the race, albeit it in an overseas country.

It was soon time for us to begin the homeward journey. Until we came to leave Beijing to return to England, Amy had been quite happy to travel by car or by aeroplane; however, the minute we got to Beijing Airport she started to scream constantly and totally unexpectedly.

In fact, I had to sit with her on my lap for the entire journey back to London or she started screaming again – I even had to try to eat my meal whilst holding her. Even on a trip to the loo I could hear her, until I dashed out to take her from the poor stewardess who was walking up and down carrying her to try to soothe her.

I've often wondered about why Amy was so unexpectedly and thoroughly disturbed by the journey to the UK. I don't know whether she was just feeling fretful or whether she was frightened by some innate instinct that she was leaving China, the country of her birth and taking a great leap into the totally unknown.

We had caught an evening flight, so we arrived at Heathrow in the early hours of the morning and between our bags and our tired and fretful baby, I've never been so glad to see anyone in my life as I was the taxi driver who'd come from our village to meet us at the airport and to drive us to the final destination – our family home.

Chapter 3

Life In England

We walked back through our own front door after our long journey to China, only we were returning as a family of three, with our tiny daughter in tow.

The first thing we noticed was that Tessa, my sister, had cleaned and aired the house in our absence, leaving fresh flowers in the living room and that her sons, Nick and Nath – my two eldest nephews – had made a huge banner saying "Welcome Amy".

It was the middle of the night and we were all so tired that we just dropped everything and went straight to bed.

We had left the cot made up and ready for our baby in the room which had been specially decorated for her and I believe that this was one of the very few nights that Amy actually slept there all the way through the night until the following morning, so she must have felt as exhausted as we did.

The following day was one of visits; my parents were anxious to see her, as were our neighbours plus my sister and my three eldest nephews, who were all Amy's cousins.

In fact, the first week or two was very much a holiday time, taking Amy here there and everywhere, including into our respective places of work and to visit Lee's family in Southport, which was a three-hour drive each way.

I always remember that initially Amy never cried very much, although she soon learned that if she did, someone would come running and offer food, drinks, attention.

She also didn't like noise and would sometimes put her hands over her ears in a group of chattering people.

I came to the conclusion that Amy had lived in a world of comparative silence for the first year or so of her life. It is unlikely that there was very much sound or speech from the other children at the Welfare Centre, and the nannies there had too many children to attend to for very much time to be spent on talking or singing to the babies in their care.

In any case, any speech that Amy would have heard prior to her adoption would all have been in Chinese, so English, including even the sound of it, would have been completely alien to her.

It is, therefore, unsurprising that her speech development was initially behind that of other young children of her age, although she quickly picked up the universal words of "Mamma" and "Dadda".

She also quickly began to recognise the key people in her life; one day when my sister and my two older nephews were visiting, she picked up a photograph of all of us and pointed to each of us and then to our corresponding image on the photograph, including herself, but all without making a sound.

Being brought up in an extended family where all of her cousins were boys and where she was the youngest of my parents' grandchildren meant that Amy soon had to find her voice to get heard. When she was still a baby, sitting on my sister's lap, she was watching all of the boys running around and playing boisterously together and making a fair amount of noise between them all. She suddenly stood right up on Tessa's knees and started shouting loudly at all of her cousins. To be completely truthful, Amy has been pretty loud, with plenty to say for herself, ever since that occasion.

We brought Amy home at the end of June 1999 and the weather was turning hot, but I couldn't get her to drink anything apart from formula milk and small amounts of plain water, so I began to worry when she wouldn't drink very much, until we hit upon the idea of trying her with "Toothkind" Ribena.

To this day, this is still one of her favourite drinks and she has always liked all things which are blackcurrant, including jams, jellies and pies.

During the next couple of months when I was at home with her, watching Amy develop was like watching babyhood in some kind of fast forward. She learned to sit up and crawl within a couple of weeks and then started to pull herself up to standing position.

Amy also started to develop her own sense of humour – she used to love me to hide her toys and then produce them in a little pop up game of peek-a-boo. She also liked watching "Teletubbies" as a baby and used to wave to them all when the programme started.

As Amy's personality began to unfold before us, I realised that hers was a lively personality and it gave me some appreciation of how deeply afraid she must have been in her little life to have become so completely withdrawn.

I don't think Amy slept through an entire night during her entire first few months with us – she would wake up night after night screaming and literally terrified out of her brains, having the kind of night terrors no child should have and I could only hold and soothe her.

During those long nights of walking around holding Amy close and singing to her, it did cross my mind that when she was left at the welfare centre as a baby of six weeks old, it may have been at night and that however cold or frightened or hungry she was, or however much she cried, no one came to her until she was found the next day.

I took to lying in the bed in the spare room with her until we both fell asleep, so that she wouldn't feel alone. I used to lay her across me, with her head on my shoulder, and her feet used to reach the top of my waist. Now when I look at her, I can't believe she was ever as little as that.

When I went away for a night for a conference for work, about a year after we got Amy, as soon as the lectures were over at 6pm, I went to my room, ran a bubble bath and called room service for a pot of tea and some fresh sandwiches to be delivered to me.

At about 7.30pm, I got into bed and stretched out as far as I could, taking up almost all of the bed, before sleeping for twelve uninterrupted hours. I still recall the sheer bliss of it and I awoke feeling more rested than I had in years.

The next day, some of my colleagues said that they had been looking for me to invite me to go out to dinner with them and then to visit some bars. But so far as I was concerned, I had already spent the most delightful evening I could think of.

It didn't bother me in the slightest, by the way, that unless it was for work (because I had to), I practically never went out at all without Amy, particularly in the first few years. After all, I had been in my thirties by the time we brought Amy home, so I had had plenty of opportunities for going out by that time and had spent none of my previous time being a mother. So the choice was an obvious one to me.

Besides, having already lost a year of her life in the welfare centre in China, Amy had such little time to be a baby, so I wanted to make the most of it for both of us.

Amy was also initially frightened of water and absolutely terrified of thunderstorms. Although Amy can't remember anything from the time she lived in China, the flooding of the Yangtze must have made a very deep impression on her because water really did mean a very changed world to her and I think that had had an impact on her at a subconscious level.

She is still fearful of thunder storms and doesn't like swimming in the sea when the waves go over her chest.

I once had an argument with a welfare visitor who told me that I should just leave her crying in her cot to get her to settle down. My answer? That it was my sleep which was broken and that Amy had been frightened enough in her young life already, so she wasn't going to be frightened in our house.

This was the same welfare visitor who told me that Amy had been so badly damaged due to the way her babyhood had been spent that we'd never be able to do anything with her. As I was holding her and my tears were falling into her thick black hair, Lee told me that she was a complete idiot, because she'd insisted on asking about our own genetic conditions, although we'd told her that our daughter was adopted, so that anything to do with our own respective genetics simply couldn't apply to our daughter. So from then on, we gave ourselves permission to disregard her comments.

(By the way, this was also the welfare visitor who took a totally opposing view when she visited us a year later and pretty much asked me what I'd done that Amy had grown so pretty and happy and healthy. My reply was that we'd loved her, paid her as much attention as we could, looked after her and fed her properly. I was only glad that Lee was with me on both occasions otherwise I would have begun to doubt my own sanity, such was the complete change in her attitude.)

We had initially asked for some help from the local welfare office because Amy would sometimes hit herself quite hard or would even butt her head hard against us. I could only imagine what her treatment in the welfare centre in China must have been like to cause this behaviour, with all the babies and young children crowded together without adequate care or supervision.

At first when she went to sleep, Amy would hold her hands firmly clasped together, with her arms close to her body, as though they had been tied together. When she was awake, she would also play little games with her fingers to amuse herself, as this was clearly the only stimulation which had previously been available to her.

Gradually, with gentle care, attention and proper stimulation, Amy's behaviour began to stop and she began to take an interest in what was around her.

I also wanted Amy to learn to trust me and to realise that I had come into her life to be her mother, so to love and care for her, putting her needs before my own.

When we first got Amy, she didn't put her arms out to be picked up and cuddled, perhaps because there hadn't been any point before. One day after we'd been home a few weeks, she spontaneously put her arms up round me, laid her head against my chest and hugged me very tightly.

I knew then that we had made a huge breakthrough in our relationship.

During those summer days, we played with Amy in the garden, we took her to the park and to the shops, while she got to know her new family, including her cousins – her oldest cousin Nick, who was then ten years old, used to push her all over our village in her pram.

It is true that I really do have the coolest five cousins in the world, who are all boys and who are all older than me.

I can't remember Nick pushing me round in my pram that summer, but I do remember that I've always got on well with him and that before I started school, I always wanted to marry him.

Now we're all grown up, I can only say that I always did have great taste in boys, even when I was little.

My next cousin down, Nath, remembers bathing me when I was a baby and dressing up to make me laugh. And my third cousin, Ben, used to like giving me a bottle.

The youngest two, Laurence and Henry, are close to me in age, so they were very little themselves when I was a baby.

It's great for me that my cousins are all now my friends as well as my family, which will last for the rest of our lives, I hope.

Amy still wouldn't chew her food very much, so I used to liquidate her meals, which I used to prepare from scratch, dredging my mind for almost-forgotten information and recipes from Domestic Science lessons at school. I would virtually tip the food down her throat to make sure that she was properly nourished.

I also gave her a bottle of formula baby milk every night until she was three years old, as I was so afraid that she would never overcome the deficiencies in her diet as a very young baby unless I made sure that she was well and nutritiously fed.

Amy never was a child who ate very many sweets, chocolate or ice creams, but she has always enjoyed her food and could be a bit of a crisp fanatic, if I'd let her.

Once when another family brought their daughter to visit us, I gave the other little girl a bottle of formula milk. Amy was beside herself with crying and kept trying to snatch the bottle away from her. At first I was puzzled until I realised that Amy may well be recalling a situation where one child having a bottle of milk meant that there wasn't one for the others. I had to pick her up and show her that there was plenty for both of them in order to soothe her.

Was I right to have taken such an almost obsessive interest in her diet? All I can say is that Amy is now a little over the average height for women in the UK, right in the middle of the healthy weight range and is rarely ill. (When she went to see her doctor over an ear infection a few months ago, aged seventeen, he couldn't find any record of her ever having been prescribed any antibiotics in her life, so I had to report that once when she was about four or five years old, she had been given antibiotics at that time, also for a mild ear infection.)

One of the things we completely underestimated when we took Amy out as a baby and as a young toddler was just how much attention she seemed to get wherever we took her; I realise that young children do attract a lot of attention from strangers, but Amy seemed to attract far more than usual. Perhaps something about her which made her stand out to the Chinese authorities, so that she was chosen as a candidate for adoption in the first place, was the same quality which drew people to her once we were in the UK.

I think it's important to record that we encountered very little race discrimination when Amy was young, either when we were out or when Amy was at nursery; all through all our lives together we have been subject to a certain amount of curiosity, however, which is sometimes covert and at other times registered very openly.

When Amy was about three or four years old and we were out shopping, we were asked by another little girl of a similar age why we looked so different, after she had heard Amy calling me "Mummy." I explained that she had been adopted as a baby to which the other little girl kept asking "But why did that happen?" until she and Amy both started clambering to go on the Tweenies ride which was temptingly located at the door of the precinct and which was clearly a distraction from the mysteries of overseas adoption.

Years later, we were visiting a restaurant in Manchester city centre, which had lights outside for decoration. As it was getting dark, Amy asked me to take her photograph framed by the lights. One of the other customers was a chap who was a little older than me and he offered to take a picture of us together. He initially referred to me as "your friend" to Amy, who instantly said "she's my Mum," causing the kindly stranger to look rather baffled for an instant before he smiled and obligingly took our photograph using Amy's i-phone.

Very recently, when arriving in Malta for a family holiday, the customs officer looked first at my passport, then he looked at Amy's and then he looked from one of us to the other and back and forth before he eventually shrugged and handed back our passports to us. He was clearly baffled that we were travelling together and that we both had the same surname of Masters.

We've just got used to it over the years.

As the long, lazy days of the summer of 1999 started to draw to an end, I had to return to work, quite simply because we couldn't afford for me not to. In those days, there was no maternity leave for mothers whose child/children were adopted, but I'm glad to note that the law has since changed in this respect.

The nursery in the village offered a place to Amy and we were glad to accept it as it would allow her to integrate with her peer group as well as being very convenient for me. I used to get up at 6am to get myself and then Amy ready so that I could drop her off at the nursery before 8am on my way to work and then collect her on my way home again, after a day in the office.

It was a nursery out of a fairy story in some ways; it was like a fairy tale house, which was, in fact, an old mission hall which had been specially adapted with lots of toys and a little garden at the back. It was a happy place with plenty of other nice children for Amy to spend some part of the week days with. She seemed to fit in there very easily almost immediately.

My days at nursery were some of the happiest days of my life. I had plenty of friends to play with – Khaerina, Tegan, Jade and Kelly – and I even had a boyfriend called Alexander.

We never had to worry about grades or doing homework and if we did fall out, we soon made friends again.

There was a different party to go to practically every weekend, as it was always someone's birthday.

Even though I had moved away from the area by the time I got a Facebook account, I made friends on it with some of the kids I remembered from nursery and I'm still in touch with most of them.

Every Christmas, we used to do a Nativity show and I remember being an angel first and then one of the kings, which I suppose was the right role for me because I really do come from the East.

There was also always a big Christmas party, with party food and fairy lights and dancing, when Father Christmas bought us all a present.

In the summer time, we used to eat picnic food outside.

Yes, nursery days were good.

It was difficult going back to work and leaving our child at nursery, but I didn't really have any choice, since my salary was needed for our family finances, despite the high cost of nursery fees. The costs were, in any case, worth every penny to make sure that Amy was safe and happy whilst we were working.

We quickly got into a routine, where we became confirmed members of the 6am club, along with many other working parents.

I think this is where I really learned to juggle different roles and to manage on limited amounts of sleep, whilst remaining functional. Although, to be honest, the first few years after we got Amy was the only period in which I can ever remember finding my career a grind and an effort and I rarely enjoyed going to work, which was completely unusual for me.

I think that perhaps my energy and enthusiasm for something had to give at this time or perhaps I was simply adjusting to different responsibilities. In any case, as Amy grew, my enthusiasm began to be regained. Although it seemed like hard work at the time, I now see that it was valuable training for me in becoming functional and multi-functional. I also learned to trust myself and to realise that I could sort out practically anything if I had to.

But I think that this period in my life must have made a deep impression on me, because at times of stress, I used to dream that I was trying to get away from work to go to find Amy, but my car and my mobile were gone and I was left trying to bicycle down motorways and up hills to get to her. Time was ticking away and I was petrified that the staff at the nursery couldn't contact me, so they would call the police and social services as it was getting later and darker and I just couldn't reach her.

The dream was so vivid, but then I'd wake up and relief would flood through me, as I realised that it was just a dream and that Amy was safe, after all.

As time passed, I used to dream this less and less often, but ironically, now that Amy is practically grown up and able to take care of herself, I've had this same dream more often again lately.

I think it might be a reaction to fact that all the responsibility I had is now lifting and I can relax a little, now that my daughter is well able to take care of herself on a day to day basis and now she just needs me in the background to provide help, support and advice (as required) as well as to be her personal dictionary and bank manager.

I wonder how many other working parents report similar thoughts and experiences? Plenty I'd guess, judging from the young parents in the office where I currently work.

It's the natural reaction of any parent to be concerned about his/her child/ren and to recognise the responsibility we have all had to take on, as well as enjoying the happy and the fun times together.

And so the days of our lives passed, in work and nursery, home and chores, outings and play, treats and holidays, Chinese New Year and Christmas.

We had to prepare two reports to send to the Chinese authorities to provide information over how Amy Tong Fang was settling into her new life in the West.

The first of these had to be sent after she had been adopted for six months and the second was at the anniversary of her adoption. We prepared each of the reports with care, providing all of the requisite information, which we supplemented with additional information, including photographs of Amy Tong Fang with her English family and in her new home.

We had to arrange for the reports to be translated into Mandarin Chinese and one of Lee's colleagues referred us to a lecturer in Chinese Studies at Birmingham University, who is Chinese by origin himself. He completed the translations for us and refused to take payment from us on either occasion because he told us that our daughter was his countrywoman and he was glad to do what he could to help her.

We were touched by his attitude, which confirmed our view that we had encountered some very kind people throughout our quest to find our daughter.

Each of the reports was sent at the due time via the UK authorities to those in China and after the second report had been sent off at the end of our first year together, we never heard anything further from the adoption authorities in either China or the UK.

I remember a swing, a slide and a sandpit from the garden of the first house we lived in and the blue sofas and the rug on the floor in front of the fireplace, where we used to play with building blocks and my Thomas the Tank Engine train set.

I was only three when we moved from this house, so I don't remember much more about it. I think it was a nice house, but small.

We moved before my fourth birthday and before I started school to a house I described to my Nan as "that nice, bright, light house". There was a big conservatory, which I used as a toy room.

It was often untidy as I used to like getting out lots of toys at a time and scattering them around, although Mum used to make me put them back before bedtime.

By that time, I was into Barbie and I had a bedroom with Barbie curtains and duvet cover. There was also a huge rainbow painted on the wall above my bed, with some big Chinese fans – blue and dark pink – hung on the walls, so that it had both Eastern and Western influence in the decoration.

I think my favourite ever toy was a little pink dressing table with a tiny stool and a mirror, where I used to keep fake make-up and jewellery in the drawers and sit brushing my hair and putting it in slides. My Nan bought it for me one Christmas when I was nearly three; she said I wouldn't come away from it for so long that it took me the whole day to unwrap the rest of my presents that year.

I was cross with my Mum when she finally gave it away to another little girl, who was just starting school, although I was about twelve years old by then and too big to sit on the stool properly.

Whenever Mum changed her car or got a hire car, she would take me on a night ride. I would wear my pyjamas, she would wrap me in up in my car seat so I was warm and we'd go for a drive to try the car out. We used to play our favourite music as we drove along. We did this for years and we only just stopped a few weeks ago when she changed her car because I got one of my own at the same time and this time round, I drove Mum on the night ride (although she didn't wear her nightie).

I used to love going round to my Nan and Granddad's house on Sunday afternoons and staying for dinner. My cousins used to come over too and in the spring and summer our parents used to take us to the local park or play with us in the huge garden before an early evening dinner and in the colder, wetter months, we used to play games and watch films together inside.

Nan's food was lovely. She used to cook us homemade chicken nuggets and roast dinners with special cupcakes for pudding – unless it was one of our birthdays, and then we would have a cake.

Then Granddad would chase us little ones round the big tree in their front garden, chasing us one way then another, while we were giggling with excitement.

Then it was time to go home for a bath and then to bed with two stories before sleep.

I used to call my Mum's mum "Super Nan" because she had six grandchildren including me and I called my Dad's mum "Special Nan" because I was her only grandchild, so she was special to me.

Dad would take me to see her for the whole day, one Sunday in every six weeks or so, when we would go out for a Chinese meal and Special Nan would play tea sets with me.

She built me a wonderful three-storey dolls' house and decorated it herself; I've still got it.

When she died, my Dad found amongst her papers that she had ordered a handmade, wooden rocking horse to be made for me for Christmas, which would use almost all of her savings.

He asked the makers to continue with it, as she obviously really wanted me to have it, and it was hidden in the garage for two days before Christmas Day.

I had lots of fun playing with it when I was little and I'm still fond of it. I've looked after it, so that that one day my own children will be able to enjoy it. My Special Nan's last present to me.

I was lucky to have an extended family to grow up in, who have always loved and cared about me and I never felt different at all.

I'm not even eighteen yet, but I know that this is how I want to bring my own children up one day, by creating lots of nice memories for them, because this feels like a special time in my childhood where I will always feel happy and safe.

When Amy was still in her pushchair, we went up to Chinatown in Birmingham, as Lee wanted to have some acupuncture treatment on his back.

Whilst he was in the Health Centre, Amy and I looked around the shops – it was just before Chinese New Year at the beginning of February and we bought a few bits and pieces to make a card and to decorate the table for a festive meal.

When we returned to the Health Centre, Lee's appointment had over-run so we were invited to wait for him in the centre's waiting room.

One of the female doctors who had come to Britain from mainland China only a couple of years before came to talk to us; she was asking me about Amy and I was explaining which part of China she was from and how she had been born near the Yangtze River when it had burst its banks.

I was speaking about Amy's birth parents and explaining that when she was left at the welfare centre in Tong Ling, she had been approximately six weeks old and that it made me think that her Chinese mother must have been in circumstances where she had had no other option than to give her daughter up. After all, no one has a baby and then keeps her for six weeks before leaving her, other than in a dire situation, which I said I believed must certainly have been the case.

I was speculating over what had happened to Amy Tong Fang's parents, when the doctor cut me short and immediately retorted, "Forget them – they're gone. Your daughter will have a good life in the West now."

I was initially shocked by her reaction, which seemed so final, but after a little while, I realised that China was then a country in which to survive itself was no certainty, so in order to do so, there was no scope for the sentimentality of looking at the past with longing or any amount of regrets, which people in the West are sometimes inclined to do; otherwise, in China, you might actually not have survived at all.

It was a salutary lesson in the importance of moving forward.

When I was in Year 2 at school, we all had to write about of our first day at school. In my account, I wrote: "On my first day at school, I was a bit upset."

The teacher, Mrs Gordon, started laughing because what really happened was my Mum and Dad got me all dressed up in my smart new uniform and they both took me to school. Then when they took me into my classroom, I just screamed the whole school down.

I wouldn't let go of my Mum, so Mrs Gordon ended up taking me off her and walking up and down with me to soothe me, while the other girls went into Assembly.

I cried a bit on the second day at school, but after that I was fine.

My teacher, Mrs Edwards, was also the Head of the school and she was my favourite teacher ever, so I soon got to like school.

There were twelve other girls in my class and we used to go to each other's parties and round to each other's houses for tea on Fridays.

After school finished, we could sit down and have tea together which was squash with bread and jam or peanut butter, then play until our parents picked us up to go home. This is how we found out that I was allergic to peanuts, by the way.

We also used to have dance classes and then riding lessons when I got a bit older, after school lessons.

The school had its own swimming pool and I find it hard to believe that I was ever really frightened of water, because for as long as I can remember, swimming has been one of my favourite exercise activities. I even learned the butterfly stroke when I was little, which is supposed to be hard, and I taught it to other younger girls when I changed schools to move to Wales.

There were a few bitchy girls at school when we got older and one of them used to love to take the mickey out of me over my middle names, Tong Fang.

That is, over my Chinese names. I never told any of the teachers about this, or even my Mum until after I had left the school, because I didn't want the girl to have another go at me. Some of the other girls also kept out of her way because she used to say nasty things to them too.

There was a boarding secondary school across the road from the first school, with girls from all over the word, so apart from that one girl, I don't remember anyone being racist to me.

Although there was some falling out between us girls, I liked most of the others and the teachers were all fine. In fact, some of the bigger girls used to make a fuss of me and ask if they could take me out with them to the shops and into the village after school. They weren't allowed, though.

My absolute favourite thing at that school, ever, was the dance shows that the dance teachers helped us to put on every year. All the girls from reception to sixth-formers were in the same show. There was a ballet scene followed by a show of different modern and tap dance routines, based on a theme in the second half.

None of the parents were allowed to see any of the rehearsals, which went on for about six weeks, so it would be a big surprise when the shows were put on for two nights at the end of the Easter term. My Mum used to come to one show with my Nan on the first night and she used to come to see it again on the second night with my Dad.

The dance teachers expected a lot from us all, but it was also tremendous fun to be in these shows. Everyone said how good the shows were and some of the older girls even won places in dance companies, as the quality of their dancing was so good.

There are two performances I remember dancing in the best: firstly, one of the ballet scenes, where my ballet class made up a chorus of little frogs and we did a special dance, hopping around.

The second was a tap dance routine, where we little ones all danced in a line as soldiers. I still have a photograph of me wearing the costume.

I also liked story time in class and I tried to learn my spellings every week.

But I've never, ever liked maths, and I still don't.

We sent Amy to a private school when she was four years old for the simple reason that the classes in the village school contained thirty pupils each and I was concerned that she would get overlooked.

I knew that if she felt overwhelmed or lost, that she wouldn't make any kind of fuss or even misbehave, but that she would just withdraw into herself again as a protective mechanism because this had worked for her before in far more extreme circumstances.

Given all of our efforts to break through to Amy, I really think that if she had withdrawn again, this would have broken my heart.

We were not especially wealthy, so it meant that we had to work hard to pay the school fees, but the reward was that she seemed to settle in well and was described by the school secretary as a "happy little soul" around the school.

Again, Amy got a great deal of attention from the older girls at school, who used to buy her extra Easter eggs and Christmas presents as well as letting her join in their games. This was a bit of a double-edged sword, because it also caused some jealousy and resentment from some of the other girls in her own class, especially when they were all first in school.

After Amy had been at school for about a year, she suddenly had a dawning realisation from listening to the other girls that she had a Chinese mummy and daddy out there somewhere, which made her different from all of the other girls.

I spoke to the teachers at school and none of the comments seemed to be at all nasty. Some of the other parents were naturally curious about Amy's origins and so were the children. I really believe that it was the first time Amy had actually understood the concept of being adopted, despite the fact that we had always been completely open with her about everything.

She would come home in tears each afternoon for a few weeks, wanting us to find her Chinese parents so that they could come to the UK to live next door to us, so we could all be together. Amy never once said, interestingly, that she wanted to go back to China herself to live with her Chinese parents there, while leaving her life in the UK behind.

She also went through a phase of telling me that I couldn't tell her what to do as I wasn't "even her real mother".

We tried to explain how difficult things had been in the part of China where she'd been born during the Spring of 1998 and that her parents had had no choice, that they had not been able to care for her, that they were needed to help regenerate the area and that China was their home.

We have always tried to bring Amy Tong Fang up to have respect for herself and others and particularly to have respect for her Chinese parents. I have always felt that fate has bound me up very strongly with her mother in particular. How can I feel other than very deeply towards the one woman in the world who has given me my greatest joy, which at the same time, is also her own profoundest sorrow?

I must be clear over the fact that I never wanted to search for either of Amy's parents when she was a child, either in secret or openly.

If I had done so without her knowledge and later revealed this to her, how would she have ever trusted me again? And I know for sure that she has learned to trust me implicitly over the years.

If I had openly searched for them, she may well have been subject to constant let-downs and even, supposing, by some miracle we could have found them, I think it would have torn Amy apart to have had two families with quite literally half the world in between them, from two completely different cultures.

Over the years of her childhood, Amy's views about trying to find her Chinese parents have fluctuated. Once she is eighteen, I am happy to respect whatever decision she chooses to take, knowing that this may change yet again as she gets older and one day has children of her own.

Our Family Photo Album

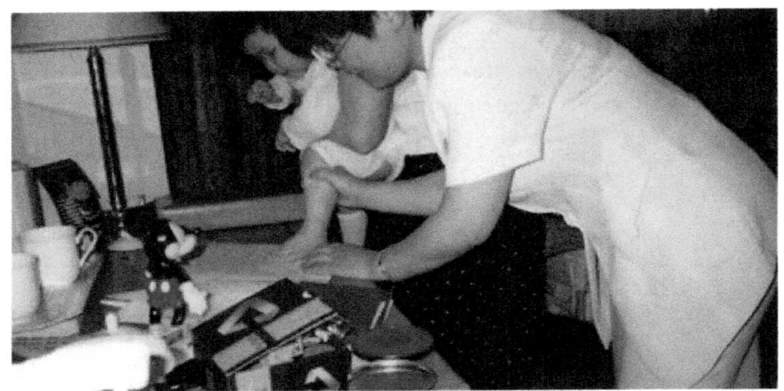

Amy 'signs' the papers with a footprint

Amy with her English Mum on the first day

Amy looking happy with her English Dad

Amy in the garden at the very first house

Amy on her first day of school

Amy with her 'Special Nan' on the dolls house

Amy's last school photo

Amy ready for her school prom

A recent photo of Elaine and Amy

I remember being sad and crying because my Chinese parents couldn't come to live next door to us and because I never saw them.

I really missed them and although I didn't remember either of them at all, I felt like there was a great big hole somewhere in my heart.

I told my English Mum that it would make me feel better if she bought me expensive presents or let me ride my bike all around the house.

If I felt annoyed with her, I also used to tell her that I was going to go back to China to find them, but I never got further than the bottom of the garden, before I came back.

One thing that helped me was that I had a Chinese friend called Adele, who'd also been adopted from China and was living with her English parents. She was a few years older than me. She used to hold my hand or put her arm round my shoulder and tell me that she felt sad too, but that you get used to knowing that you miss your Chinese parents and that you learn to manage without them.

One of my friends from school, who was very sensible, also used to tell me that no one had two sets of parents, so I shouldn't feel so bad not to have that either.

My Mum used to sit stroking my feet (soft, so it tickled, with her nails) while we watched TV together and she would make me her "special" sandwiches, which I still love, or she would sit reading to me when I was cuddled up in bed.

My favourites were Laura's Star, where a little girl finds a broken star, which she mends and returns to the sky, or Mary's Secret, where the little girl's Mum has a secret which goes round the whole school.

We used to talk about my Chinese parents sometimes and about what might have happened to them and why they hadn't been able to care for me.

I think these things must have soothed me, because I don't remember feeling sad for very long at a time and it was only every now and again when I thought about my Chinese mum and dad that the feelings of loss and sadness would come over me.

The holidays were always difficult, trying to find childcare, so I could continue to work, but we managed it between us – one summer with the help of a friend's grown-up daughter, who was in college, training to be a nanny and then with the help of a fully qualified nanny, we "shared" with another family, whose daughter was at Amy's school.

In any case, I used to try to arrange something special for every holiday and we would sometimes go to stay with my parents for a few days in the May and October half-terms (February half term was always my least favourite of the school holidays) at their holiday cottage in Lincolnshire.

Skegness was close by and Amy used to love the beach. In October she would splash in the waves in her Wellington boots; there were three separate sets of donkey rides on the beach and we used to walk up and down the promenade so she could ride on her favourite donkey from each group.

They all belonged to the same owners, who had won an award for having the best-kept donkeys in Britain.

We would also buy wristbands for the funfair, where we could have as many goes as we liked on the little rides for the whole day.

The funfair at Skegness used to open every Easter and Amy's birthday was often in the Easter holidays. One year, she asked her Nan to check the date the funfair opened and she was so delighted to find out that it was on her actual birthday.

She excitedly told her Granddad that she could hardly believe that it was her birthday, so she was going to get cards and presents and a birthday cake as well as it being the first day of the funfair. She ended by saying, "Just how lucky can you get, Granddad?"

My Dad gravely replied that he didn't think that Amy could possibly get much luckier than that.

I truly think that the visits to Lincolnshire were amongst the highlights of the earlier parts of Amy's childhood.

I loved going to Nan and Grandad's cottage in Lincolnshire. I liked the funfair and the donkeys, as well as the beach and paddling in the sea.

Mum and I used to play a game where she pretended to be turning a skipping rope for me while I jumped the waves and while we recited the "Teddy Bear, Teddy Bear" skipping rhyme.

I also liked visiting the windmill at Alford, where Granddad would help me climb to the top, so we could see the views before having lunch at the little café in the grounds.

I liked going down to Falmouth on the train too with Mum to meet Nan and Granddad, who also had a flat down there.

We used to stay at the Falmouth Hotel and use the swimming pool before breakfast, then we'd go on the putting green while waiting for Nan and Granddad to come and take us out.

There were also holidays with my cousins in Spain and one year to Tenerife in the long Summer holidays.

I still love Skegness and I'd like to go back there soon.

I'd also like to go back to Falmouth, but it's taken me a little while to think this because when Granddad died about five years ago, Nan sold the flat and for a long time, I know it would also have made me too sad to go back to Falmouth.

But I miss it and I now think it would be nice to go back to visit some of the places I went to with Nan and Granddad.

All the places Amy and I went together and all things we've done show that we got on well together, but it makes it sound as though we never fell out or that Amy was never in trouble.

It seems only right to say that were times when we were all trying to get ready in the mornings when Amy would refuse to co-operate or I'd be running late and we'd bicker.

It's also true that there were times when she'd try to play me up and start having a tantrum if she couldn't have her own way; in fact, Amy has always had a quick temper, where she will quickly get angry and just as quickly it will all blow over. (I often used to say that I'll pity her husband, when she eventually gets married, because one minute she'll be all charm and the next, she'll be in a huff, without him even knowing why or what he's supposed to have done.)

Our social worker, Rob, had told us that very often adoptive parents don't feel like they have the right to tell their child off, or that they think they shouldn't say or do anything which might upset the child, because they are trying to compensate for what has happened prior to the adoption.

Initially, I also experienced these feelings towards Amy, but I eventually realised that I had to be firm with her when she misbehaved, or she would end turning into a spoilt brat, whom nobody would ever want to be around. I was also alive to the fact that however much I was sensitive to what had happened to her when she was a baby, the rest of the world wasn't going to take this into account for the rest of her life. In effect, the world owed her nothing, so it was very unfair to her to bring her up as though she must always be tiptoed around.

Once when she played up in a shop, I just refused to talk very much, which really upset her. I told her that I was just so sad that I had a little girl who couldn't behave any better than that, so I had nothing to say. That had more effect than anything else, perhaps because Amy realised that she'd gone too far with me.

I overheard her talking to one of her dolls one day and she was saying, "Now it's a long time since you've been in real trouble and not been allowed to watch the Disney channel, but you're going the right way about this happening again very soon now." And yes, I did instantly recognise myself in the "mummy" voice.

I think that I've been a very soft parent in many ways and I still run round after Amy a great deal, but I've always been strict over things like manners, having consideration for other people and sitting down properly to eat at meal times. I sometimes wonder if her upbringing has been a bit old-fashioned because I was in my thirties when I got her.

Of course there have been occasions when Amy has been naughty for me – I could stand and bawl at her when she was a little girl with less effect than either her Dad or mine simply saying, "Now what is all this, Amy?" – but she has never had a school report that didn't describe her as "delightful" somewhere in it.

And she's visited the homes of plenty of school friends over the years; many of them have said that she's welcome to visit anytime, because she behaves herself and has very nice manners.

I can only say that although Amy had her moments when she was little, it was usually only for me and I'm glad that it was that way round. At least it meant that I could always unhesitatingly take her with me whenever we decided to go anywhere as I knew that she would behave herself when we were out.

I'm not sure if I remember Mum getting cross with me particularly when I was little. I remember her saying that I couldn't have friends around to the house again if all I did was to show off, but that might have been when I got a bit older.

I know I've got a quick temper and if someone upsets me, they really know about it.

And I still hate it if people ignore me when I'm in a strop. My cousin, Ben, did this to me once at a festival when I was a teenager and I went and sat in the car on my own.

He still wouldn't come and find me so I had to go back to the camp to find the rest of them, when I'd calmed down. I wasn't best pleased, but he just laughed at me, so I pretty much had to get over it.

We used to go out with Nan and Granddad quite often when I was little and Granddad would never put up with bad manners. He used to pay me plenty of attention and do fun things with all of us cousins, but only if we behaved ourselves and I don't remember him telling me off. Ever.

So I don't think I can have been naughty all that much at all really and I never got in trouble at all with the teachers at the first school I went to.

The first year Amy started school, my sister was thinking of emigrating to South Australia, where we had an uncle and a host of cousins, so she decided to visit before arranging to make her home there with her two sons.

It had been more than twenty years since my sister and I had last visited Australia, so the idea of meeting her out there over the Easter holidays (my only way of getting three consecutive weeks off work) grew more and more appealing.

In the end, I booked last minute flights for Amy and myself, with a stop off in Los Angeles on the way back, but the booking was so late that I had to pick the tickets up at the airport, as there was no time to get them delivered to me.

We had already secured an apartment with a balcony right on the beach front at Glenelg, within walking distance of the trams to Adelaide.

My sister and her two sons never did get as far as Australia on that trip – they got to Los Angeles where they decided to stay for a few nights before returning home because they found the entire flight all the way to Australia too long and too tedious just for a short holiday.

Amy actually had her fifth birthday while we were on the aeroplane, flying somewhere over the Far East, but as we had taken a night flight, we both slept for large parts of the journey, with Amy curled up in her seat, covered by a blanket, waking up from time to time for meals, drinks, stories and a few games.

I set off with my tiny daughter one April day in 2003, we boarded an aeroplane in the evening and when we woke up, we were on the other side of the world.

I've never quite gotten over what a wonderful feeling this gave me and how it made me realise that the two of us could go anywhere together and that we could accomplish whatever we set out to do.

I've looked at the photographs of the first time we went to Australia and I can't believe that I was so tiny. The photos show a little girl, in summer clothes and different sun hats.

I used to climb on a chair on the balcony of the apartment, so that I could see over the top of it and look at the beach and the sea at different times of the day.

I really liked the apartment, which was big and cool and on the long promenade along the beach front. There was a Jacuzzi bath, which me and one of my second cousins put bath foam in, so that the bubbles went right over the edge of it and all over the floor.

Recently, some of our family visited from Australia and they asked me if I could remember them from when I visited when I was little. I could remember some of them, but not all of them, as we have quite a lot of family living in Adelaide.

I went to feed kangaroos and a koala bear called Holly, who turned up in some of our games and stories for a few years afterwards. One of my distant cousins, who was strong and about twenty years old, dangled me high above a snapping crocodile until I squealed.

I've been told by a few of my Australian family that when the time came to go home, I didn't want to leave.

The following year, we went to Hong Kong for a visit, where we went on trips to look round the city, including a visit to the famous Stanley Market, where I bought presents to take home for my friends from school, but I thought the weather was too humid for me.

I also didn't like some of the food and I actually got sick one of the days, unusually for me. When my Mum and I went for a posh Chinese meal on the second day we were in Hong Kong, we recognised hardly any of the dishes on the menu, including from when we'd visited Chinatown in

Birmingham and Liverpool. I suppose this shows how much the food is changed to suit Western tastes.

In the end, we ordered chicken bird's nest soup as a starter, which was brought to our table in a big golden dish and presented to us with a flourish. Once it had been served to us, we both tasted the soup, but neither of us liked the taste of it, which was very strong, so we managed to swallow a few mouthfuls each and left the rest of it.

I think we might have offended the chef and the manager at the restaurant because we ended up getting quite a big bill and Mum said she felt she had to leave them a pretty big tip, as she felt bad that we didn't like the food there.

I remember seeing lots of girls all dressed up in the city, who were queuing up to get into nightclubs and I really wanted to go into one myself to see what they were like; but as I was only six years old at the time, I didn't get to do this.

To be honest, I prefer Australia to Hong Kong and I am saving up to go back there for a visit with one of my friends as soon as I can get the money together. Some of our family who live in Australia have already told me that we can stay with them anytime we want, especially as their own children are now grown up, so they have plenty of room.

I remember being my Uncle Peter's bridesmaid when I was seven and I had to carry the wedding rings across the beach in Hawaii. We went to his wedding and back in a white stretch limo and I'd never been in one before or been a bridesmaid until then.

I wore a beautiful cream dress with flowers on and I had some silver sparkly sandals. I had my hair specially arranged with flowers. Uncle Peter gave me a Hawaiian necklace to wear.

I've still got the dress and the necklace, but I don't know what's happened to the shoes.

On the way out to Hawaii, we went to New York for a few days. My favourite part was going round Central Park in a horse and carriage and then visiting the little zoo there.

On the way back to the UK, we went to San Francisco, and during our visit when we went out for the day to Fisherman's Wharf and to see San Francisco bridge, I tripped over on the beach and fell over into San Francisco Bay, landing down on my bottom. My Mum picked me up and laughed.

It was so sunny, my clothes soon dried out while we were listening to street entertainers before we caught the tram back to our hotel, which I loved. (We saw a newly married bride in her dress with her husband, who were both riding on the tram.)

Lee came with us on the trip to the USA, the year my younger brother got married and it turned out to be our last ever holiday as a family, because shortly after that Lee and I decided to separate.

Although some of the above paragraphs sound as though Amy and I were always holidaying together, the truth is that these are the events which stand out the most and very much of our lives – like everyone else's – was caught up in a round of caring for our daughter, hard work, household chores, paying bills.

The decision to split our family up was a mutual one between Lee and me; we had already started to lead separate lives whilst living in the same house, so we decided to call an end to our marriage whilst we could do so amicably and before either party started to treat the other badly.

We parted as friends, as the most important thing for us to remember was that we are both Amy's parents and that we both still have her best interests at heart, so that even if our marriage has ended, we can still remain united as her parents.

Of course, I felt very guilty that Amy was to be subjected to being from a family where the parents had separated from each other and I dreaded telling her of the decision.

As it happened, she seemed quite excited by the idea of having two different bedrooms, in two different houses, like some of the other girls in her class at school.

Even at the school her teacher and head teacher informed me that if I hadn't told them of the separation, they would never have guessed it from Amy's behaviour.

The only thing that changed for Amy was that her Dad moved out of the house to a smaller place a couple of miles away and, in any case, Lee came to the ex-marital home to see her after work a few nights each week and she stayed in her bedroom at his house every other Saturday.

Amy just seemed to take the change into her stride. It's easy to imagine that for her, the change was a very small one in comparison to the experiences she had already lived through in her young life.

Or maybe it's just that children are more resilient than we, as adults, imagine.

Did the social workers make a mistake by letting my English Mum and Dad adopt me, just because they later got divorced?

All I can say is that I don't remember being upset by them splitting up very much at all. Occasionally, I missed Dad being around all the time, but I was generally just getting on with my own things.

I love them both and I still see and contact my Dad, even though I've always lived with my Mum.

I think I've had a nice childhood and I want to have a good life as a grownup.

And I really don't think I would have had much of a life if I'd stayed in China, a country where I don't know where I could have gone once I got too old to live in the welfare centre. I only know that developing physical disabilities and mental health illnesses was very common in children brought up in these centres.

That is, if I had even lived to grow up. The welfare homes full of children in the 1990s hadn't been called "the dying rooms" for nothing.

So for me, there was no mistake and I can only ever be glad that my parents were allowed to come to China to adopt me and to give me a loving home, even if my home changed a few times while I was growing up. I just know that I was really, really lucky to be given the chance to have a life at all.

Whatever else I have or haven't been lucky over during my life, I have always been fortunate over the choice of my career, many years earlier.

It has provided me with a reasonable, independent living over the years and has allowed me to provide for my daughter.

Of course it was hard work, looking after a young child and running a home while working full time, but when I became a single parent, the benefits of my previous working life became apparent.

Shortly after Lee and I decided to separate, I got head-hunted by an organisation which specialised in personal insolvency. My new job allowed me to stay in the former marital home, as I was able to take on paying all of the household bills and the mortgage. Rather than paying me any maintenance, Lee continued to pay Amy's school fees, so the initial disruption to her was kept to a minimum.

My new job involved over an hour's commute to work each way every day and would involve working long hours some days. I was already accustomed to my day beginning at 6am and commuting some distance to work. The major difference was that I was used to leaving work on the dot so that I could rush to pick Amy up from, by then, the after school club.

I was already having to "nanny share" for the school holidays, which I could no longer afford and Amy was, in any case, starting to resent that style of care now that she was getting older.

The obvious solution was to recruit an au pair, to do the school runs and to act, generally, as a mother's helper to me, as well as to provide cover for the school holidays when neither Lee nor I could get the time away from work.

It was the only way I could realistically continue to work – part time work was never considered to be viable by employers in my profession and the idea of not working was simply never an option at all for me. I hate being told what to do at the best of times, so the thought of the welfare state doling money out to me and telling me how much I was allowed for which items of my expenditure was not something I would ever have been able to live with.

As it happened, we managed to find a lovely twenty two year-old au pair from the Czech Republic, who lived with us for almost two years and who truly became like one of the family during this time.

She could drive and one of the purposes of her coming over was to improve her English, so we registered her on a local college course. Her English also improved considerably during the time she was with us, by day to day use and practice. The young lady, Vladi, now has her own home and a little son, having returned to the Czech Republic some years ago.

I was responsible for her keep, paying for Vladi's college course, providing a car, with a reasonable allowance for petrol and for paying her an allowance each month. In return, she would generally do both school runs for me, provide Amy with her tea and make sure her clothes were clean and ironed, as well as cleaning the house and preparing some of the family meals. She even baby sat for me a couple of nights each week by prior agreement!

In many ways, my life was the easiest it had ever been since I'd had Amy, as I was able to delegate some of my day to day responsibilities; although my day still started at 6am when I'd get up to get myself and Amy ready for work and school respectively, and ended when I finally got to bed at about 11pm, at least I didn't have to do all the running round in between.

As Lee also had Amy every other weekend from Saturday night to Sunday lunchtime, I was able to go out again sometimes and I began to develop a little social life of my own for the first time in years.

Of course, it was also a tremendous responsibility in other ways, because I had to work even harder to pay all the bills on the house, plus pay for and run two cars, as well as supporting two dependents, one of whom I also had to pay a well-earned allowance.

Before I started my new job, I remember waking in the nights and going downstairs to make tea. I would pace the kitchen, worrying over whether I was doing the right thing by leaving my previous secure employment. I was conscious that if I messed things up, it would badly affect both Amy and Vladi, as they were both relying on me absolutely to provide for them both and to be the sole head of the household.

In the end I came up with a useful analogy: about a year before, when we had gone to Cornwall to meet up with my Mum and Dad, we'd gone to a park with miniature world statues. In the grounds had been a ride called the "Bat Rider", which children over six years old could go on with an adult. You had to climb a very high tower, then cross a high walkway to come down a huge spiral on a swing. Now I have always been petrified of heights, but Amy wanted to go on the "Bat Rider". We duly climbed the tower and Amy almost ran across the high walkway to the other side, where I stood, hesitating. I realised that I had to get across to her, so I began to walk across the divide, very determinedly, telling myself to keep going and all would be well, if I just didn't look down to see how high up I was.

So I decided that if I just kept looking forward and getting on with my new job, all would be fine; I just mustn't stop to think about everything and how much responsibility I was taking on, in case I spooked myself.

So that's exactly what I did: I just carried on without, metaphorically, looking down and our household, with the three of us, was a happy one during the time we all lived together.

That's not to say that there weren't some difficult and trying times though. There was one occasion where Amy was ill for once – she had a sore throat and earache- but I had to be at work for a meeting with a team of lawyers over a serious staff issue, which had been arranged several weeks in advance, so I really needed to go in.

As I went to leave for work, Amy was clinging to me, asking me not to go and Vladi had to peel her off me, which made me feel truly wretched. I burst into tears as soon as I got in the car to drive to work.

I rang Lee and as his Court appearance was a short one that day, he called at our house as soon he had finished. He telephoned to tell me that had looked through the window and seen Amy lying back against cushions on the couch, laughing with Vladi at something on the Disney channel and sipping a drink. When he came in, she began groaning and telling him in a faint voice about how ill she was.

Lee waited with her until I could get home and assured me that she was fine, in fact well enough to go back to school the next day.

Not that any of this mattered. I still felt that I was failing as a mother and as a professional; in fact, I wondered how I'd ever fooled myself that I could manage to juggle both as a single parent, when Amy was still so young.

But this was really an isolated situation and we "girls" mostly had lots of fun together.

Very first of all, I had to get used to Vladi and I think she had to get used to living with us, in a different country. But it wasn't very long before we got on well together. She used to make me snacks after school and take me and one of my friends to the park or on trips in the holidays.

She also used to watch my favourite TV programmes with me, like Animal Hospital, and we would sing along to the theme tunes together.

Vladi and one of her friends came to London with me and Mum, so we could all see the sights. The two au pairs stayed in with me one evening while Mum went out with an old friend for dinner, but then Mum and I went out together during the other evenings we were there, while the older girls went to clubs and bars. I remember us going to the theatre to see "Lion King" one of the nights and getting a taxi back very late to the apartment where we were staying.

Vladi came to Cornwall with us too during the first summer, but it rained most of the time, so she didn't get to see very much, which was a shame.

I even got to have a puppy called Lucky at long last, a little while after Vladi came to live with us, because it meant that we wouldn't have to leave a dog alone in the house for most of the day any more. I was so happy because I'd wanted a dog for ages.

Then one of Mum's friends, who she hadn't seen very much of for a few years, got back in contact with her. She had a daughter who was a year older than me and they both used to come round to our house or go out with us.

One weekend, they went down to West Wales and asked us along. At first we said we couldn't go, as I was supposed to be going to stay at Dad's, but as he was ill, so I couldn't go to his house, we decided to go after all.

We set off after the others. As we didn't know the way, I ended up map reading for Mum, in the dark.

I was eight years old by this time.

We arrived there late and we went to a party in a forest, where everyone sat round a bonfire, as it was fireworks night. I don't think that Mum knew the rules, though, because she turned up in high heels, a fake fur coat and with a bottle of champagne, which made walking through the dark forest very hard for her. Our Welsh friends still tease her about this.

The man who gave the party ended up becoming my stepdad, but I didn't have any idea about that happening then. Mum didn't either.

We just liked how friendly everyone was and how nice it was to go somewhere we'd never been before.

We went back to stay in West Wales a few times over the winter. As we saw more of Cardigan Bay, we liked the beautiful beaches. Our very favourite is one with a natural waterfall, which you can walk behind when the tide is out. We also liked the little town and villages by the beaches so much that Mum rented a house right next to the beach for us for six months, so we could go there for weekends and holidays or whenever we wanted to, taking my puppy with us.

There were plenty of children who lived near the beach, who all knew each other and who were keen to play with me. Mum let me go to the beach or for ice creams with them after one of the neighbours told her to stop worrying. Everyone kept an eye out for all the children to make sure we were all safe and they all knew me and which house I was from.

I used to love going down to the beach on sunny afternoons and climbing over the rocks or paddling in the sea.

This is how we came to visit Wales and how we came to love it and to make friends here.

Chapter 4

Life in Wales (1)

One of the reasons I liked going to Wales from the very beginning was because my Mum let me go out with other children my age far more than she ever did in England. I was only ever allowed to go out round the group of forty houses where we lived and I wasn't even allowed to go to the village shop just down the road, even with a friend, although I didn't have to cross a road.

The main road through the village there was always busy and there were plenty of lorries thundering down it every day.

I'm not sure if my Mum was scared that I'd be in an accident or get kidnapped or something. Anyway, I wasn't allowed to go very far at all without a grown-up with me.

I also liked the beaches at Cardigan Bay and to start with my Mum's friend and her daughter, Jenna, came to live in the house we'd rented as they wanted to move to Wales.

So when Jenna started at the village school, we started to get plenty of new friends to hang round with.

My Mum also made friends with some of the people we met on our first visits down there.

I liked Wayne, the guy who gave the party, and his friends Sandy and Martin plus his wife Jo. It was always a good laugh visiting them or going out with them or having them round.

I liked Wayne to start with; I wasn't sure I liked the idea of him being my Mum's boyfriend though, which was what happened as we got to know him.

He could be great fun and he also had a cute little Jack Russell dog called Stumpy, so I got used to the idea more, I suppose, as I saw more of him.

Wayne was different to any other people that I'd ever met as he used to have wooden swing boats, which he'd take to festivals during the summer. The first year we knew him, Mum and I would meet him at different places each weekend during the summer holidays.

The very first festival I ever went to when I was nine years old was a small one. There was some rain during the weekend and I remember running round with some of the other children who were there. We were playing and rolling in all the mud.

I wore my pyjamas for the whole weekend and I remember getting so muddy that it was even in my hair.

When we got home, my Mum ran a bubble bath for me and dumped me in it, still wearing my pyjamas, to give me a good scrubbing.

Wayne used to take a wheelbarrow to the festivals with a blanket and if I got tired at night, Mum would put me in it and Wayne would wheel me back asleep to our camp.

We used to stay in a truck which was shaped like a gypsy caravan, with bunk beds and a little kitchen, where Mum used to cook food we'd brought on the way down. It was fun to stay in there and to go to different festivals at the weekends.

When the summer holidays were over and it was time to go back to school, we carried on going to the house at Cardigan Bay, which we still really liked. It was like going on holiday whenever we went to stay there – except that we had to keep going back to England again after a very few days.

As I continued to see my Dad every other Saturday night, we got to go down there every alternate weekend and some parts of the school holidays.

In any case, every Sunday evening when we had to pack up and go back to England, I used to wish we could stay there, even if it meant I would still have to go to school there and not just give up school altogether (as I first thought).

I started to nag Mum about us living at the house we'd rented in Wales all the time and moving from England, but she'd say it wasn't that easy for us just to move.

Maybe it was my nagging or maybe it's because Mum can sort almost anything out when she thinks about it enough, but about a year after we first went to Wales, she said it was all fixed up and that we could move down there to live if we still wanted to.

We moved just in time for Christmas and started living in our house at the beach overlooking the sea at Cardigan Bay all the time. On clear days, we could see dolphins swimming in the sea from our living room window and we took Lucky to the beach on Christmas Day. We were the only ones there.

Our visits to Cardigan Bay really were relaxing for both of us and it was such a beautiful place that I also wanted to spend more time there, which is why I decided to rent a house there, right at the beach.

Also, Amy had just got Lucky, her puppy, so it would have been impractical to have gone away on holidays, especially while he was so young and mischievous, so our "holiday" house was instead of us going anywhere else that year.

I found it a peaceful place and I was at a time and a place in my life to value finding peace, both with myself and with my surroundings.

I felt as though I had spent ages working on the "ready, steady, go," running around working hard to pay all the bills and to support us, taking on responsibilities for me, Amy and Vladi. So the house in Wales also became a place of refuge as well as rest to me.

It was essentially also a place of escape for me and I've always been someone who has a tendency towards escaping – if my life is not going a way that I like, I find a way to change its course, even if that includes moving geographically.

Amy's right and Wayne did become my boyfriend, although I didn't expect to fall in love or to find a permanent new partner at that stage in my life, so I was rather caught by surprise myself.

As we still lived in England for the first year, meeting Wayne at festivals or when we went to Wales or if he visited us occasionally in England meant that our relationship was initially more of a developing, rather than a sudden thing, so I think Amy gradually got used to the idea of having him around. It meant that she didn't have to share me all at once and that there were, initially, plenty of times when it was just the two of us. Even now I've re-married, I still find time for Amy and I to do things on our own, although now, inevitably, she's the one who's getting too grown up to want to do many things with me very often anymore.

When she first came up with the idea of us moving to Wales, although I also liked the idea of moving there permanently, I just couldn't see how we could manage to do it on a practical level.

Cardigan Bay is a tourist area, so the work opportunities there are strictly limited. There was absolutely no prospect of me continuing in my profession, unless I commuted for several hours each day to and from Swansea or Cardiff.

Firstly, I considered, if I did decide to move, one of the reasons would be to avoid lengthy, daily commutes and, secondly, the salaries which were quoted to me would have involved me taking a substantial pay cut.

We weren't rich, but I had worked hard to obtain my position, so I was reluctant to take any sort of backwards step. In any case, I couldn't really afford to do so, now that I was Amy's key provider.

One of the things I was the least worried over when contemplating a move to West Wales was over the local schools – because the area was a rural one, the class sizes were all small compared to English schools, including the secondary schools, where the form sizes comprised less than twenty pupils for each class.

The secondary schools are also truly comprehensive too, insofar that the pupils were from a variety of different backgrounds, unlike England at the time, where pupils went to school almost entirely by their postcode.

I came up with the idea of approaching my employers to find out whether they would be prepared to let me attend the office for three days each week, whilst working from home for another day each week, meaning that I was paid for four days' work each week.

As I was prepared to cover the same amount of work by working for longer hours on the days I was in the office, whilst being paid for only four days, I had the basis of a deal.

Although it meant that I would still have to take an appreciable pay cut, I would no longer have the expenses of maintaining an au pair, including the costs of running an extra car.

I also figured that the change to a more relaxed way of life was worth it, as we had enough money to live on and I was completely able to support my daughter.

In any case, now that Amy would no longer be at private school, Lee began to pay some maintenance to me.

By this time, Vladi was no longer living with us and her replacement had been with us for six months; she decided that she wanted to stay in the UK for a further six months, so we helped her to find another family.

Lee was concerned about us moving so far away from where he lived, but we agreed that he would have Amy to visit regularly for weekends and that she would spend part of the school holidays with him. I realised that it was a little hard on him, although he had moved on by this stage and was leading his own life.

I have to give Lee a great deal of credit and to say that he took the decision for us to move to Wales with good grace, although this was a considerable personal sacrifice on his part, as the arrangements for him to see Amy now had to be more regimented. I know that he misses her, but that he was prepared to put her wishes before his own.

At the time of the move, I couldn't afford to keep paying for the house in England anymore, so I decided to rent it out to cover the costs of the mortgage, while continuing to rent the house at Cardigan Bay.

I realised that I was keeping my options open here a little bit, because we still had a base to return to if we decided that moving to Wales was a mistake, at a later date.

That was when I began to lead what even I can only describe as a mad life: my week would begin when the alarm went off at 4am on Monday mornings when I would get up, quickly get dressed to drive for five hours, across five counties to get to the office by about 9.30am where I would work until 7.30pm. I would drive to a local inn for supper, where I would stay the night, before getting up for breakfast to be in the office again from 9am until 7.30pm, when I would go back to the inn for supper, to get up early to be in office for 8.30am to leave at 4pm to begin the five hour home journey back to Wales.

Although the travelling sounded quite a lot, I was already commuting for an hour each way every day, anyway, so instead of travelling each day, it was simply the same amount of time, but just compressed into two very long journeys.

In those days, my work/home life was divided into two distinct parts, allowing me to focus fully on each one. So however mad it sounds, there was actually a certain logic to the plan I had formulated.

And when I used to get to the coast road, which was the final stage of my return journey, where some parts of the road are high so I could see all around the coast line, it was so beautiful and peaceful that I would know that our decision to move to Cardigan Bay was all worthwhile. Sometimes, I would see the moon reflecting in the water and sometimes I would see the sun gradually sinking into the sea.

I would feel myself almost visibly relaxing and I have never grown tired of these views, however many years I pass this way, week after week.

I have to confess though that whenever I got back home late on Wednesday nights, I was usually wired-up and over-tired; Wayne or Amy only had to look at me the wrong way for me to over react, so I adopted the practice of having a cup of tea and going for a bath to try to wind down.

But afterwards, it meant that I had four long days to spend with my family in a lovely place, where we could spend quality time together.

The primary school I went to when we first moved to Wales was a tiny school, close to one of the beaches – we had to pass two beaches on my way to school and then back each day. There were only about fifteen of us in the whole school from all age groups, with one other girl who was the same age as me.

There were two class rooms with two teachers and one lunch time assistant, who had worked at the school for about thirty years. When I left, she bought me some stationery, which she said she's done for every child who'd been to the little school to take with him or her to senior school when the time came.

We used to play games in the little playground and the older pupils like me would help with the younger ones.

My Mum used to leave for work while I was still asleep on Monday mornings and then she would get back on Wednesday evenings just before I went to bed.

She would usually leave me a note at first and later she would send me a 4am text message to wish me a good week. She would also ring home at 6pm on the two nights she was away, as she was always still working away in her office at this time in the evening.

I didn't mind my Mum working away for the first part of the week, which is, in any case, the boring part of the week, as I then had my Mum around all the time for the other four days. I didn't want her to give up work because then we'd have no money to pay for what we wanted and it was better than her working every day like she did in England, dashing home in time to help me with my homework, then getting me ready for bed with half an hour for chats and a story before I went to sleep, then having to get up really early every day to get herself ready before getting me up and ready for school. This way I had loads of time with her at the end of the week.

Although Wayne still had his own place, he used to spend almost all of his time with me and Mum; I had spent more than a year getting to know him, when we still lived in England, but I got to know him better while Mum was working away because he used to take me to school on Mondays, Tuesdays and Wednesdays, then meet me again. We often used to take the dogs to the beach on the way home, before we went home for him to fix my supper.

He used to fit his own work around this until Mum came back at the end of the week, when she would do the school runs; she would take me out after school or let me have friends round for tea on the days she was at home.

To be honest, to start with I did resent Wayne being my Mum's boyfriend a bit and I didn't always like him telling me what to do or telling me off, but he could also be good fun and he used to do more adventurous things with me that Mum would never have let me do, like the time he tied a sledge to his four-wheel drive and pulled me fairly slowly along an empty, snowy road.

So I soon got used to him and sometimes I even resented Mum a bit for taking his attention away from me from when she came home. If I fell out with Wayne, to start with Mum would end up trying to referee between us both, but after a while, we'd both end up turning on her instead. Most of the time though, we all got on well enough and had a pretty okay time together.

When I was due to leave to go to the local senior school in the town, the tiny school that I was attending was told that it was due to close down as there were not enough pupils to keep it going. So the last few weeks that I was there were spent on outings to use up all the money in the school fund.

The same year, I was allowed an extra week off school so that we could go to the festival at Glastonbury to work by picking up litter. Mum and Wayne took a caravan to stay in and I took a little tent which I pitched right next to it.

Because we were working there, we got our food provided at one of the canteens and our camp was pitched at the edge of the festival, where there was a block with proper showers and flush toilets which were cleaned regularly.

Mum and I thought that it was worth working there just for this, particularly as the week went on.

We stayed there for just over a week in total, so I got to watch the festival site made up from the beginning and then taken back down at the end.

We would get up early in the mornings, go for breakfast then get dropped off in the village of Glastonbury. Mum and I would do the litter picking in the village and around the lanes each day, along with some of the other ladies in our camp. We are still in contact with some of them.

Although we were working for our ticket and our food, we still had plenty of time for Mum to take me to the kids' field and to see all the headline groups that I wanted to see in the evenings.

In fact, I so much like going to festivals that I will be going to the one in Reading this year with a group of my friends (boys and girls). We all also go every single year to one of the smaller family-run festivals, which we've gone to every year since we met Wayne, although he no longer works there.

I would also go and stay with my Dad in England on a regular basis and ever since we moved to Wales, I have spent alternate Christmases divided between my Mum and my Dad.

Mum and Dad usually used to meet at the halfway point of the journey, so that I could continue to go to stay at my Dad's house for the weekend or for some part of the school holidays after we'd moved like I used to when we lived in England. I used to go more often when I was younger. As I've got older, though, I've started doing more and more things with my own friends rather than with either Mum or Dad.

I've taken some of my friends to stay at my Dad's house with me and I have met up with some of the girls I went to my first school with, while I've been staying at his house.

I've always kept my life with my Mum and my Dad separate from each other, although they have both told me that they are friends now, so there is no reason for me to do this. It's just something I've always done, is all.

Anyway, I have special things that I do with only my Dad, like stopping for fish and chips on the way back to his house after my Mum has dropped me off, and going for Sunday lunch at my favourite Chinese buffet-style restaurant. I usually go to stay with my Dad around Chinese New Year, so that we can go to Chinatown in Birmingham to see the celebrations and to have Chinese food.

Just before I went to senior school, I went to China for about three weeks with my Dad, as he had a Chinese girlfriend, who was about my Mum's age, that he had got to know and visit regularly.

They decided to get married in China, so I went over there with him for the wedding. I was a bridesmaid.

My stepmother, Ning, is from Guilin and while I was over there, I met her family and visited their houses. They all made me feel welcome and I know that they would let me stay with them again if I ever wanted to.

I liked my new stepmother and both she and her family have always been very kind to me.

Dad says Guilin is in a completely different part of China to Tongling, where I was born. It is situated on the Li River and the scenery around it is very pretty.

We didn't get the chance to visit Tongling while we were over there and I didn't want to, anyway, because I was visiting China for the different reason of my Dad's wedding. This was nothing to do with my birth or adoption and I didn't want to mix up the reason for my visit for my Dad's wedding with something completely different.

Dad, Ning and I went on a few trips together while we were over there. I kept a scrap book, which I still have, of my visit, including the wedding and the places we visited.

I had a good time over there and it was interesting to meet Ning's family, but I was also glad to get back home again at the end of the trip.

It was completely irrational of me, but I felt quite bereft seeing Amy going off with her Dad for the trip to China; perhaps because three weeks seemed such a long time for her to be so very far away, and also because we had never been apart before for more than about a week at a time.

I have to admit that I was upset too by the idea that when Amy was with Ning and her Dad, everyone would think that Ning was her mother.

Of course, I realised that it was only fair to both of them that Amy should go to China with her Dad so that they could spend some time together; it was also a great opportunity for Amy to visit the country of her birth, not just as a "tourist," but also to meet a Chinese family whom she now had connections with and, of course, I didn't let her know how I felt as I didn't want to spoil things for her.

It was also important to both of them that Amy should be at her Dad's wedding and that she should get to know her stepmother. And I knew that Lee would, of course, take very good care of her.

Amy emailed me every few days and, as it was clear that she was well and enjoying herself in China as well as spending time with her Dad, I was very glad she'd gone with him, although I couldn't wait for her to come home.

In any case, I had plenty of other problems to concern me around this time, as the organisation where I worked was itself in financial difficulties; most ironic for a company whose prime business was that of insolvency practitioners. As a senior member of staff who held cases in my personal name, it was not possible for me to just find a new job, as I had professional obligations which caused me to stay to see how this would play out.

The uncertainty of my employment position continued for several months, which was rather stressful, until things came to a head and the company employing me entered into a formal insolvency process. It had been a constant worry to me over what would happen and it looked as though I was very likely to be made redundant. With a young daughter to support in addition to all the household costs to pay for, I knew that I would have no choice other than to start looking for another job as soon as possible.

As ever, I was very lucky in my career and I was the only one of the four insolvency practitioners to be taken on by the organisation that took the business over on a reduced basis. I have remained in employment there ever since, although I soon became required to work between two different offices during my three days per week in the office, which has entailed getting up at 4am on Mondays to get to the Midlands office, spending one night in the Midlands, then getting up early the next day to travel to Manchester for two hours, before working a long day in that office, staying overnight to return to work, before the long drive back to Wales in the early evening.

Travelling over five hundred miles and then working for 28 hours within three days was rather demanding, but I disciplined myself to do it every week, come rain or shine, snow or wind.

As well as working from home on the other two days, I also began to take my laptop on holidays with me and to catch up on correspondence over the weekends on occasions when we were particularly busy. Rather than finding this a grind, unlike the days when Amy was a baby, I began to relish the challenge and the extra responsibility I was being given.

Perhaps it was because Amy was getting older and the care she required was not constant or perhaps it was because I was able to re-assert my own identity again.

After all the years that have passed, my role as an insolvency practitioner has now become part of my persona.

In any case, the change in my employment was favourable to me and it has provided me with the completely independent means of providing for my daughter over the years, for which I will always be thankful.

I never knew until ages later that my Mum had only kept her job by the skin of her teeth round about the time that I first went to secondary school. She didn't tell me about it at the time because she didn't want me to worry about it.

I started at the secondary school in the town, where there were four forms in each year – two which were Welsh speaking and two which were English speaking. I went into one of the English speaking forms and there were about fifteen of us in my class.

I had to catch a bus to and from this school every day, but it was really easy because the bus had to go past the house we were renting, so if I stood at the bottom of the drive in the mornings, the driver would pick me up from there and then drop me off at the bottom of the road on the way back.

There were quite a lot more girls than boys in my year and throughout my time at the school, there were lots of fall-outs amongst us girls. One of our head of year tutors said that he had never known a year like it.

Until I started at that school, I had never heard swear words used on a regular basis, particularly in school, before, although I have to admit to getting in big trouble with both my Mum and my Dad over my own use of bad language a couple of years after we moved to Wales.

*Although one of the girls at my last school had laughed at my Chinese name, I had never been called "Chinkie" before. Most of the others weren't racist towards me. There was one boy when I first started at the school and later one of my so-called friends used my race as a way of insulting me, by calling me a "Chinese c***" when she fell out with a group of us.*

One of our little gang included a boy who was two years older than me and he knocked on the door of her house and complained about her behaviour to her parents. It was awesome, as they didn't know what to say when a teenage boy calmly told them that what their daughter had just said was completely unacceptable.

Amy told me about the boy who used to call her a "Chinkie," but as this was outside of school, I couldn't really complain about him to the head teacher or the head of the year.

I did tell Amy to keep away from him as much as she possibly could, since he was clearly being brought up to be a racist and that his comments were more of a statement about himself and his family than they were about her.

I believe that after a while he got fed up with the taunts and just stopped.

As for the girl who called Amy a "Chinese c***," her mother telephoned me as she was concerned that her own daughter was being picked on! After a full and frank discussion, I went round to her house to discuss things and she apologised, admitting that she was ashamed of her daughter's behaviour.

In the end, the two girls actually made friends again and over the years since this incident, this particular girl has, in fact, since shown herself to be a loyal and affectionate friend.

As we progressed through the school, I fell out with one of the other girls, who sent me a message on Facebook calling me a "Chinkie." My Mum and Wayne reported this to the police, who came to take a statement from me. They then went round to her house and warned her that racism is a crime in Britain. The police told me and my Mum that if I hadn't answered her back on Facebook, they would have charged her and she would have had a criminal record.

Her email also said nasty things about how I was adopted and that I didn't even know who my family were and never would. Most of my year were shocked by her comments and told me to reply that at least my family wanted me, unlike hers who probably wished that they'd never even had her.

It feels really horrible to be taunted anyway, but it feels even worse for someone to use an insulting name about your race as a way to hurt and humiliate you. As for using the fact that you are adopted, well that's beyond anything I can describe really, especially as there was nothing you did to cause it and there's nothing you can ever do to change it.

The reaction of the others in my year made me realise that this was just a particularly mean girl and the only time my parents had calls from the school was about the problems I had with her. So after a bit, I decided that she was the one with the real problems, not me.

I have to admit that I got my own back on the mean girl in the end, anyway. Most of the girls at school really fancied at least one of my cousins when they used to come and visit. This girl fancied two of them at different times and after she was so hateful to me, one of them came to visit us.

We all met up at the same sixteenth birthday party and she was really trying to get with him. He just made it dead clear in front of her and the rest of us that he would NEVER have anything to do with her, especially after what she had done to me. It was just so incredibly cool. Karma's a bitch sometimes and it's well worth waiting for.

The other pupils were fine and they didn't say racist things to me. I had friends I used to hang out with at breaks and lunchtimes. We had fall-outs from time to time, but then so did loads of the others. Once we got into our teens there were regularly girls falling out, being in tears and sometimes even fighting. I'm afraid that our year was well-known throughout the school for all the bickering and falling-outs amongst the girls.

Girls in my year regularly had to go the room we called "Space," which was a sort of time-out room to cool down.

Most of the time I didn't mind going to school, even if I didn't really like school work and although there were a few times when I was upset about something, it wasn't anything major, except for the really mean girl, because I can't even remember now what some of it was all about.

Yes, I well remember the incident with this particular girl, which just couldn't go unreported, even if only to force both the girl and her parents to realise that this kind of hurtful and malicious behaviour is totally unacceptable and that it's deeply hurtful to be on the receiving end of it.

The police contacted us to make a statement and Amy showed them the messages that she had received. They had no hesitation in going straight round to the girl's home, where she was given a warning in front of her parents.

I said that I was happy enough with this, as it was clear that Amy had retaliated to the comments made to her.

We received no apology from either of the parents or from the girl herself at any time and I told Amy to delete her from Facebook and to just ignore her as much as possible.

I was actually contacted by the head of the year from the school over the incident as this had led to a certain amount of friction in the year, as the girl felt that she was being marginalised by the others and a group of them, including Amy, had to go to see some of the teachers.

I did point out, in a perfectly calm manner, that the school had never had to contact me before in connection with Amy, that there seemed to be number of incidents surrounding this particular girl and not just with Amy from their own account, so the source of the problem did seem rather obvious.

I added that Amy was, in fact, the aggrieved party as the police incident showed, that the other girl was clearly being "sent to Coventry" as a result of her own actions, and that I had told Amy to keep well away from her, as she was clearly trouble, but that this could only work if the teachers undertook to keep the girl away from Amy too.

I have to say that the head of the year did sound rather nervous during our conversation, but I never heard from the school again while Amy was there and this particular girl did not make any further taunts or racist comments that we ever found out about.

I had a group of friends I used to hang out with most of the time, although some of my friends changed as I went through the school. We used to go to the park together and to the cinema as well going to the beach on warm days.

My Mum always used to let me do something special for my birthday and she let me invite a group of friends to come with us, so sometimes we went to the cinema and then out for a meal or to the waterpark with all the slides and a wave-machine with supper afterwards in the café at the back of the fish and chip shop in town.

We always had great fun and some of the girls would come back to my house for a sleepover.

I used to go to Youth Club with some of my mates on Thursday evenings, as the youth leader was Bernie, one of my Mum's friends, so Mum could meet us afterwards at 9pm to drive us home.

Mum and Wayne always let me invite friends round to the house at the weekends or Mum would drive me places to meet them, so long as she knew where I was and what we were doing.

I'm still friends with some of the boys and girls I was at school with, but some of the others, I just see around town to speak to every now and then. This is what seems to happen once you leave school and everyone starts doing different things.

One of the things I regret was that I didn't keep up with my dancing when we moved to Wales, although there was a dance studio in the town which Mum said I could go to. I now wish I'd agreed to go to there.

I did keep up with my horse riding for a while, but after I started to get older, my social life sort of got in the way at the weekends so I don't do that anymore either as I don't really have time for it.

So overall, most of my later childhood was pretty much like that of lots of other adolescents living in a small town in Britain.

When we'd first moved to the house we were renting in Wales, I'd been renting out the ex-marital home we owned in England, which meant, of course, that we could move back there any time we wanted to without too much inconvenience, so we had a sort of safety net, as it were.

About fifteen months later, however, the landlord's agent served notice on me to quit the property we were renting, which forced us to take the decision of whether we wanted to sell up and buy a place in West Wales or whether we wanted to return to England, since there didn't seem much point in renting a place while we were renting out the house we owned. In effect, the time had come for us to decide if we wanted to move to Wales on a permanent basis or not.

It would mean that I would still have to do the weekly commute to England, but if we moved back to England to live, I would, in any case, have to go back to a daily commute. We'd settled happily into our lives in Wales, so we decided that it was time to sell the house in England and to move permanently to Wales.

So I made arrangements to sell our house in England as soon as possible, as the spring and summer months would prove the best time to sell it. Of course, I had to give notice to our own tenants in order to do so; they were unexpectedly difficult at first, as they initially wanted to buy the property themselves for considerably less than the asking price and I couldn't afford to do anything other than to refuse their offer.

We were lucky in that we found a purchaser for almost the asking price of the property very quickly. The only drawback was that they wanted the property by a certain date in the summer, so that their children could get into the local schools in September. So I decided just to sell the property and once the sale was complete, to find a house to buy, rather than complicate things by trying to buy and sell at the same time, in case the sale fell through due to missing the requisite completion deadline.

In the meantime, our tenants found a property which suited them, so we ended up with a situation where the tenants moved out one Friday and the purchasers moved in exactly one week later, which couldn't have worked out any better for us all if we'd deliberately planned it.

Once we had ended the notice period at our beach house (which was itself eventually put up for sale by the owners, but not until we had actually gone to the inconvenience of moving out of it, which completely put me off purchasing it from our former landlord myself) we agreed that we would all go to stay at Wayne's place, to allow our property sale to complete and to allow us to look for a property suitable to be our new, permanent family home in West Wales.

Once we had sold the house in England, I knew that it would be much harder to move back there again, especially as I don't believe in moving backwards, but only moving forward, so we had now committed ourselves to living in Wales.

Life in Wales (2)

We went to live at Wayne's place at the very beginning of the summer, at the end of my first year at senior school. The weather was warm when we moved there.

Where he lived was like nowhere I'd ever thought of living before. To start with, it was in the middle of nowhere and you had to go down a long, very narrow track just to get there.

The house itself was just a little wooden cabin, with one room and a bedroom with a shower. The water from the shower was from rainwater which had been collected. This was actually nice to shower in.

The only electricity was from a generator and we had to light a log burner to keep warm. Oh and there was no flush toilet, so we had to go outside to a shed where there was a compost toilet. My bedroom was a caravan which was next to the cabin.

There was a lot of land around the cabin and Wayne used to keep hens in one of the fields. We also had a baby orphaned lamb called Stella, which I helped to feed with a bottle at first. There were no neighbours nearby, but lots of high trees, so when we were there, it felt like we were almost on our own in the whole world.

The lamb grew up with our dogs, who used to run up to Mum when she got back from working away as a sign that they were glad to see her. Stella also started running up to Mum and she would jump up to her, as soon as Mum got out of the car. This was great when she was still a baby, but as she got bigger, she would run up to Mum and put her front paws on Mum's shoulders, nearly knocking her over. Mum said that this was quite scary, particularly after a long journey.

Sadly, Stella just disappeared one day when we were all out and although we all looked all over for her we never did find out what happened to her, so this has always been a total mystery.

Wayne had stopped doing the swing boat rides at festivals, but he had one festival he wanted to go to that year so he could meet up with his old mates, so he went leaving me and Mum at home to look after the animals.

He explained to us how to light the log burner and to work the generator, but we didn't really listen. As soon as Wayne set off, Mum and I got our things together, then we drove down the coast road, where we checked in to one of the posh hotels, with our own balcony and Jacuzzi. There were also two swimming pools, so we spent the weekend relaxing and having long baths, with delicious food served to us by room service, so we could eat on the balcony overlooking the sea. We even had one of our favourite meals, which is a very posh afternoon tea, served to us on the terrace. The lady on reception looked puzzled when we checked in and gave our address, which was only a couple of miles away.

We went back to Wayne's place every morning after breakfast, to let the chickens out and to feed the animals and again in the evenings after supper to put the animals away. On the last evening, we drove down to put all the chickens away for the night before we went to bed.

When we arrived at the field where they were all kept, we were surprised to find that all of the hens and the cockerel had escaped from their field and that the hens were all over the place. Some of them were even up in the trees.

We did our best to entice them down with food, but we only managed to get two or three out of the fifteen or so hens to go into the hen house. One of them was sitting on top of it, but she just wouldn't come down. We couldn't see or hear the cockerel anywhere.

It was getting darker and colder outside, so in the end we just closed the hen house door to keep the few hens that were inside safe for the night and we drove back to the hotel. Mum and I both felt really fed up that we had spent so much of our time driving about over the weekend to see to the chickens when most of them had gone missing in the end, anyway.

The next morning we got up a bit later and had a leisurely breakfast at the hotel as we were in no real hurry to rush over and feed three chickens. As we approached the hen house, we were both really surprised as we could hear the cockerel crowing from inside.

When we opened the door, the cockerel came out followed by all of his ladies, apart from the one who wouldn't get down from the roof of the hen house. We never saw her again, so maybe a fox got that one, as there were plenty of foxes in the fields around. We used to hear them at night and they would set our dogs off barking.

Me and Mum were both really creeped out as we have no idea how the cockerel or most of the hens got back into the hen house after we'd left the night before. I guess it was just one more mysterious thing about that place.

It turned out that it had rained at the festival Wayne was at, but the weather was beautiful all weekend where we were staying.

This was our very successful attempt at surviving basic living conditions on our own, which we both really agreed had turned out to be a pretty cool weekend.

Once our house in England was sold, it was starting to get to the end of the summer and the weather would soon be starting to get colder, so it became clear that we couldn't continue to live up at Wayne's place, because I wouldn't be able to keep sleeping in a caravan with no heating in the autumn and winter.

Also, it was miles from the town, so although it was okay in the summer, we knew we had to move as soon as we could buy another house.

So we started house hunting before I went back to school in September.

It was certainly an experience living at Wayne's place. Despite some of the inconveniences of living there, it was a beautiful place – peaceful and secluded with a timeless feel about it. There was also a definite mystical atmosphere to the place, so it was not wholly surprising that some mysterious things happened while we were living there.

Initially, we thought about buying it between us and re-building the cabin, but if we had done, Amy and I were also planning to buy a "regular" little bungalow about a mile away, with all modern amenities, such as electricity, running water and heating, so that we could keep escaping back to it.

I have to confess that neither of us seemed to be made of the stuff required to "live outside," as I used to term it, as we are both too keen on our basic comforts to be any kind of pioneers.

In the event, the prospective purchase came to nothing, so Wayne continued to own his acres of forest and in the end I bought our current property, which was a two-bedroom bungalow with an upstairs dormer room, which was built in 1930. It had a kitchen and bathroom which had been added to the back of it, which were both rather poky and the entire house was in need of quite a lot of modernisation.

The property was set on an acre of land, although at first this was hard to discern as the grounds were full of trees (after which the house was named) and hedges.

After some initial redecorating, the house was habitable and we moved in during the autumn, while Wayne started to clear the house and to remove all the hedges at the front, which had overgrown and which made the front rooms of the house too dark, because they were blocking most of the natural light.

It took an entire year for us get planning permission to knock down the kitchen and bathroom, so that we could build a new kitchen which was more than half the existing downstairs floor space, with a bedroom over the top of it (with an en suite shower room) making the existing upstairs room into a landing and another bedroom. We also had a new downstairs bathroom put in plus we knocked the dining room and sitting room into one large living room.

The only rooms which remained the same were the two downstairs bedrooms, one of which has always been Amy's, ever since we very first moved in.

All of this sounds quite simple when I list it out, but actually it wasn't. To start with, we had to live in a caravan across the village for about four months over one winter, because the house was uninhabitable whilst most of the major building works were carried out; but at least this time we had running water, with a flush toilet and a shower, and electricity plus heating by way of Calor gas fires and oil fired radiators. There was even a washer dryer we could use in a next door outhouse.

We had building contractors to carry out all of the structural work, whilst Wayne and his business partner, Simon, did all of the internal work except for the electrical work, so we were able to choose our own designs inside, as well as the some of the layout of the re-designed property.

Of course there were snags, such as when the foundations had to be dug down as far as six feet, due to the roots from some of the older trees. This caused significant delays and increased costs. In fact, the cost of the whole project over ran by about twenty per cent from the initial estimates, causing me to worry over juggling the finances to get all the works completed. I felt as though I was literally wringing out every last penny from the funds I had set aside for building works and there were times when I was in despair over whether I would run out of money before the house was even habitable.

There was also a huge amount of dust, dirt and rubble involved in the renovation, which I had completely underestimated. It felt as though it took months and months to get rid of it all, even after we'd finished the house.

We were able to move back into the property after the first four months, because we had an upstairs toilet with a shower, some heating, two habitable bedrooms and a makeshift kitchen to prepare meals. After that, we literally moved from room to room (apart from Amy, whose bedroom was sorted out from the very first) as each one was renovated.

There were times when I was literally in tears of frustration over the delays and the increased costs; it truly was a case of blood, sweat and tears – the workmen's sweat, Wayne's blood and my tears.

In fact, there were times when I wished I'd never set eyes on the place and that I'd bought somewhere else to live. It's surprising in some ways that I found the whole project so difficult to deal with, considering that I had dealt with such big issues in my life before this. I can only conclude that I found some of it so frustrating because so much of it seemed outside of my own control, including the escalating costs.

I first bought the property in the autumn of 2010 and after allowing for the year's delay in obtaining planning permission, the building works started at the end of 2011. The property was finally signed off by Pembrokeshire County Council with everything done to the required standard in the late spring of 2015.

In the end, the small bungalow was converted into a sizeable 4-bedroom dormer bungalow, set in very spacious gardens, so we have finally got what we wanted.

Although the house itself is now finished, we are still working on the back garden. I think it's the kind of property where there will always be something to do here or change there, so we'll probably never quite think that it's entirely done. Our next door neighbour recently told us that he bought his own property over twenty years ago and two extensions plus some stables in his extremely large garden later, he is still working on his own property, so our own three and a half years doesn't seem so excessive after all.

Wayne moved in with us permanently soon after we got the house. We eventually succeeded in what we set out to achieve, which was a family home, located in a rural village where we all like living, just three miles from the sea side, where we don't have to lock our doors or our cars, where everyone helps one another and where we can all enjoy having our friends round to visit or to stay.

All of my nephews have been to stay here whenever they've wanted or needed to, so we have created a home which is also a place of refuge, as well doing all the things which a house should do, by providing warmth and comfort and shelter.

It's also a house where there is a little bit of all of us in it – me, Wayne and Amy. We all lived through the major rebuilding project together to create a place in which Wayne and I intend to stay in for the rest of our lives.

It will eventually belong to Amy, so one day it will be her choice over whether she ever decides to live in it and to pass it on to her own child(ren) or whether she decides to sell it, but my hope is that we have created somewhere which can eventually be passed on by her, down the generations.

After the first year we moved into the house, we spent the next few years working on it. I had my fourteenth birthday party in the newly built upstairs bedrooms before we put all the furniture back in.

Wayne and Mum arranged somewhere for all us to sit up there and rigged up some music. Mum cooked us all some supper and we had some drinks with straws. Then we had chocolate croissants with hot chocolate at about midnight, before we all went to bed. The boys slept on mattresses upstairs and the girls all slept in sleeping bags packed into my room downstairs. There were six boys and six girls at the party, including me.

While we were upstairs, Mum and Wayne also had a few of their own friends over for supper in the kitchen and from time to time, one or more of the grownups would come up to spend some time with us for a little while before leaving us alone again.

I was also involved in deciding some of the things about how the house would be. Mum let me choose which kitchen we would have and how my own bedroom would be decorated, as well as some of the carpets.

Because I've spent my all of teenage years here and because I have been happy living here most of the time, I feel very attached to my house. My pets are happy here too.

The one sad thing about moving into the house was that we had to give Lucky away because he kept fighting with Wayne's dog, Stumpy. They were both male Jack Russells and each one was trying to be the top dog. They used to fight each other from time to time, really trying to hurt each other. We always managed to separate them, but they were both often sore and bleeding afterwards. We tried to keep them apart as much as possible.

When we first moved into this house, it started out being small so they were at much closer quarters to each other than before and they began to fight more often. We were really afraid that one of them would get seriously hurt or killed.

In the end, we decided that Lucky would have to find a new home, because Mum was away for part of the week and Wayne was working locally, so he spent more time at home looking after the dogs. Poor Mum's hands were trembling as she had to sign "adoption" papers to sign Lucky over to the dog charity who were trying to find a fresh home for him.

To start with, he had to go to live in kennels, which Mum insisted on paying for, while he was waiting for a new family to take him in. As it happened, the first place he went to didn't work out, as it was with a lady and her little girl, who were both out all day. Lucky wasn't used to be being left on his own like that, so he was really unhappy. He kept pining for some company, so then he started to misbehave.

He had to go back to the kennels so that the dog charity could see whether another owner could be found for him. Eventually, two guys who live in Bristol agreed to take him and we have heard that they travel around with him in a little compartment on the front of one of their motorbikes. He has a little helmet with ear protectors and they spoil him quite a lot.

Giving Lucky up for adoption was one of the hardest things we've ever done, even if it was to keep him safe. It was so sad watching him leave, especially as we were told that we wouldn't ever be able to see him again. We had to agree that we wouldn't try to keep in touch with him, so that the dog charity staff were free to find him a place wherever they thought would be best for him and to give him a complete new start.

We only found out what had happened to him because the lady from the dog charity used to live in our village and she told us what had happened to Lucky to set our minds at rest, because she knew that Mum and I were both so upset over losing him. We both cried for a few days after he left and I felt that I had a Lucky-shaped hole in my heart for quite a long time.

I still have a small framed photograph of him as a puppy, wearing his first little collar and I still think about him from time to time. I miss him, but I'm glad that he's found new people to live with, who obviously love him.

I did wonder whether the way I felt over Lucky was just a bit like my Chinese mum must have felt over leaving me at the welfare centre all those years ago, in the hope that I would one day be adopted by people who would love me.

A couple of years later, I found another puppy in one of the barns at the festival we go to each year. She was one of a litter who were all starving, as their mother's milk had failed. So I took her back to camp and looked after her myself. Others at the festival rescued the rest of the litter and we see the other dogs every year. She was only a few weeks old then and I've had her ever since. I called her Tipsy, because she is all black, apart from the tips of her paws, which are white and the tip of her nose, which is white and pink at the very tip.

She is a cross collie/whippet lurcher and although we all love her and even grumpy old Stumpy gets along with her, she knows that she's mine.

She is so definitely my dog that when I'm out or away, she sometimes goes to my room to look for me, or jumps up onto my bed to wait for me to come home.

Despite settling in Wales, we never have given up our tendency to travel and to go different places. When we first met Wayne, we used to travel to meet him at various festivals and although he's retired from working at them now, having sold his swing boats a few years ago, we still go every year for an annual meet up with old friends and acquaintances, at one of the smaller, family orientated ones.

Over the years, most of my nephews and my half-a-nephew, George (nephew number's two's long term best friend, who has become one of the family) and my sister plus some of Wayne's family have met us there over the years. Amy has also taken friends with her, although this year, for the first time, she'll be able to go by herself with her own friends and meet with us there. Going to this particular festival, where we found Tipsy, is a regular highlight of our summer.

Three years ago, we travelled to Malta, the place of Wayne's family origins, although he had never actually visited there before. We all immediately liked it so much that it has become one of "our" places; we arranged a real five-star holiday for the three of us to go there to celebrate Amy's sixteenth birthday. Wayne even managed to locate some of his distant cousins.

The summer of 2014, when Amy left school, was long and hot, especially as Amy had finished her exams by the end of June. As a leaving school treat, I took her to London for a long weekend, when we visited the Harry Potter museum, and generally enjoyed a few days looking around the capital.

I think we've even infected our great friend Bernie, with her two children, George and Ellie, since we've been on trips to Liverpool, Manchester and Dublin together, for the two girls to go to concerts and a trip to Anfield, with a trip to Old Trafford for me and young George.

When she gets older, I hope that Amy will return to me, as a traveling companion, since we can always think of plenty of places we want to visit, maybe eventually taking her own child/ren with us one day in the distant future.

When I left school at the age of sixteen, I went to the school prom, like a million other teenagers throughout the UK. Mum bought me a champagne coloured prom dress when we were visiting Manchester, which got voted by the teachers as the second best dress at the prom. Despite there being loads more girls than boys in our year, I even got a prom date too.

After school, I started at one of the local colleges, but this didn't work out very well for me.

My Mum helped me to get a job working in Manchester, so for a while I've travelled there to work with her for three days per week doing computer support work in the Information Technology department. I really like the people where I work. And I go to night classes at one of the colleges in Wales one night per week.

It's been great experience for me and everyone says I've grown up a lot in year-and a half I've been at work, but I know it's now time for me to go back to college on a full time basis in September to continue with my education.

I'm due to sit my driving test a few weeks after my eighteenth birthday and I've already got a lovely little car which I bought with some of the money that my dear Nan and Granddad put to one side for me from when I was little, so it would be given to me when I reached the age of my majority. I got the money a few weeks early so that I could get the car I wanted, even though we had to drive all the way to Swansea (an hour and a half drive away) to get the exact car I wanted.

Once I pass my driving test, it will make me more independent and I'll be able to drive to visit friends and family to see them or to visit for the week-end, including going to my Dad and Ning's house.

So I will have enough time, money and freedom to enjoy myself for the next few years, without having to take on too many grown up worries yet, I hope.

We've been very lucky during Amy's teenage years that most of the friends she has hung round with have been nice kids on the whole. There have been a couple of girls over the years that I haven't been very keen on, because I've thought that they were a bad influence on Amy, although I have always encouraged Amy to have her friends round to the house, so that we know they are all safe. I've often taken her to places with a car full of friends and then picked them all up later.

Of course, we've had plenty of teenagers visiting and staying overnight throughout Amy's school years and I've always kept the house well stocked with food so there's been plenty for them to eat or snack on. I just had to be careful not to give all Amy's special treats away, as she likes to keep some all for herself, the result of being an only (and a unique) child, I suppose.

I think the fact we live a couple of miles outside of the town has been a factor because it has meant that Amy has had to ask me for lifts to and from town or to the nearby beach and although I've always been willing to provide them, it has meant that I've always known where she's being dropped off and when she's being collected. Living outside of the town has also meant that Amy didn't have any scope for hanging around the town until late in the evenings, especially on school nights.

Obviously, now that she's older, Amy has much more freedom and she sometimes catches the train up to Cardiff with some of her mates to go to concerts or to visit the array of shops, which are quite limited for teenagers in our home town.

There have been a number of occasions when I have been annoyed with Amy during the difficult years, almost all of which has been to do with her being in a stroppy mood or over her attitude towards me or Wayne, over her general manner, and particularly over the way she sometimes speaks to me. (That big capital "A" for Amy seems to reflect a corresponding capital "A" in Attitude.) But underneath all of this, she is still the same sweet, affectionate little Amy she always was and her manners can still be delightful, when she wants.

I know that Amy has always behaved well for Lee and Ning, which I'm glad about.

I am also honest enough to admit that she is far better behaved as a teenager than I ever was, plus being far less argumentative or downright rebellious than I used to be at her age. In fact, she's actually got a great deal of basic common sense, which seems to give her a balanced view on things.

Wayne and I finally got married in March 2015 after being together for more than eight years. I didn't want to get re-married while Amy was still in school, as I wanted us both to still have the same surname. As it turns out, I've still retained my name as Elaine Masters for professional reasons, so I am still known by that name as much as I am by my new name of Elaine Rizzo.

Now that Amy is spending less time at home and much more time with her own friends, it's strange to find that on the days that I'm not working away, I have more time for myself than I've had in decades and that Wayne and I now have the chance to spend some time on our own together, as a couple.

But this house will always be here for Amy, who will always be the child of the house, no matter how old she is. So will Wayne and I, as well as her Dad and Ning, although I think that we should still all reserve the right to tell her straight if at any time in her life she behaves in a way which we don't think is right, whether she likes it or not.

I think we've got on okay as a family most of the time over the years, although we have had our fallouts, but they never really last long. I think Wayne can be annoying, especially when he takes the mickey out of me or tries to wind me up.

And as for Mum, she has the very annoying habit of repeating things over and over, especially when she thinks you're not listening or taking on board what she's just said. It drives me mad sometimes. She can also be quite strict once in a while, particularly over what she calls my "attitude" and "carry on". She goes into what I call her insolvency practitioner mode. She's all the more scary because she doesn't shout or scream, but she speaks sternly and she says things that are so bang on that there really is no answer to them.

But most of the time we get on well and Mum always has time to listen to my problems and to drive me and friends around. She's always taking me places and finding things for us to do, when she's not working.

I actually think that she's completely obsessed with work to be honest. Not only does she actually really enjoy going to work, but she actually LIKES dealing with difficult problems and stuff, which is a bit sad. She's old now, though, so I don't suppose she'll ever change.

But I've got to hand it to her. Not only has she looked after me properly over the years and tried to bring me up to have nice manners, but she's even worked hard enough to buy the house for us all, as well as taking me lots of places and making sure that I've always had almost everything that I wanted.

I know that Dad and Wayne have both helped to bring me up in different ways and I'm grateful to both of them, but without my English Mum, I think I'd have been lost over the years. And I think I still would be.

I was pleased when Mum and Wayne got married last year as they have been together for years now and I'm happy for them both.

They had a big wedding with a pirate theme, with live music and dancing. I was my Mum's chief bridesmaid and I invited some my own friends to join in and celebrate with us. Our entire family, including all my cousins at once, my Nan, my Auntie Tessa and both of my uncles, plus most of Wayne's family all travelled from all over to come to stay in Wales, so it was a truly great weekend.

So what is there left to say? Only that we all love visiting Malta, Wayne's place of origin and where I spent my sixteenth birthday. I do still like going on holiday with them sometimes, especially if they're going somewhere that I want to go. But I also like spending time with just my friends too.

Only that I still keep in touch with my Dad and that I go to see him and Ning from time to time. We still go out to our favourite places together and visit some of Ning's Chinese friends.

Only that we have all made some great friends living round here and that I've done all of the usual teenage things while growing up, as well as being lucky enough to have spent some of my childhood years living in a beautiful place, where I also had plenty of freedom.

Only that when my Chinese mum left me outside the gates of the welfare centre almost eighteen years ago now, because there was nothing left for me in Tongling, she must have had the desperate hope that I would find a happy life with people who loved me. I can only say that her wish did come true.

Everyone keeps asking me how I'm going to celebrate my birthday in a few weeks' time. I already know. We're getting a cake made for me shaped like an 18 with my name iced on it, with some red roses for decoration, as these are my favourite flowers.

We've been friends with my Mum's friend Bernie, who is married to my stepdad's business partner Simon, and their daughter Ellie and son George, forever now. We've also been friends with Sandy whom we met on our very first visit here. We've like a local extended family now.

On my birthday they all are going for a meal at a fancy local restaurant with us. Some of my closest friends – Joe, Tom, Jodie, Chelsea and Luke – are also coming with us.

So for my 18th birthday, I'll be getting cards, presents, some money, a birthday cake and going out to celebrate with my Welsh family. Just how lucky can you get?

And so to now

Amy is about to become a legal adult and although plenty has happened to us in our lives, the time really has passed quickly and it doesn't seem like more than twenty years has now passed since the very start of the story.

Despite the inevitable ups and downs, I have always thought that I was lucky to have Amy as my daughter and I've never taken having her for granted for even a single day. I know that being allowed to adopt her is a privilege which I was fortunate enough to be granted.

Before we adopted Amy, we were asked by our social worker about what our hopes for her were. My wish was that she would be happy and that she would have the courage to deal with life's challenges. Photographs of her, from when she was little, show her that she looked a happy child and recent photographs of her show that she is a still happy person. And as for her courage, well, I think our story speaks for itself.

We've done so many things together and I've always believed that Amy and I truly were destined to be mother and daughter, as the old lady in Tiananmen Square told me many years ago – after all, science can't explain everything.

I only have to consider the very circuitous route by which we became mother and daughter to know that it wasn't just a question of sheer chance.

I lost my chance forever of being ordinary when I miscarried my son; Amy never had a chance of being ordinary almost from the time she was born. But we each survived and we have continued to more than survive over the last almost seventeen years.

Lately, I was also told by a gypsy that we have an unbreakable mother-daughter bond and that anyone who tries to get between us will find him/herself firmly dumped on the outside.

Whether you believe such statements or not, this has indeed proved to be the case with me and Amy over the years.

I am honest enough to admit that I am proud and astounded by our achievements as mother and daughter – the woman who was told that she would never be a mother and the tiny baby we were told was so badly damaged we'd never be able to do anything with her.

Our two voices, which have told the same story, will start to tell our separate stories because my daughter has grown up and will now, inevitably, start to lead her own life away from me, as all children must.

I only know that whatever happens to each of us as we go forward, our lives will always be closely intertwined and the bond which has been forged between us over the years will always be unbreakable.

My Mum and I have done some amazing things together – we've travelled all over the world together and completely rebuilt our house, which are the most obvious things. And we've had some fun.

But the most important thing is that we've always been there for each other.

We both know what it's like to have lost members of our family and those we've been close to, but this has drawn us closer together over the years.

I don't think there's very much chance of me ever finding my Chinese mum (or dad either). I've realised lately that I don't even know if I want to look for them now, although Mum and my stepdad and my Dad and my stepmum have all told me they will help me, when I'm eighteen, if I want them to.

I just don't want to build my hopes up again and again, to get let down if I can't find any trace of my Chinese parents.

In any case, if I ever could find either of them, I know that they'll never come to live in Britain and I'll never ever go to live in China, so I'd end up having to leave them all over again. Which I think really would break my heart this time round.

I don't ever want to live in China again because I've lived in Britain and been a British citizen since I was a tiny baby. I've grown up here with the only family I've ever known.

My home is in Wales, so although I might leave and spend some of my life away from here, I know I'll always be able to come back to the house that we three (me, my Mum and Wayne) rebuilt together. This is where I'm really from now, in my heart, even though I've still got my copper medal to remind me of my birth place.

I think that one of the best things for me is that, as well as my parents, my extended family of my grandparents, aunts and uncles and especially my cousins all made me feel like I belonged with them.

Of course I feel deeply about my Chinese mother, who gave birth to me and who is out there somewhere on the other side of the world. But I don't want to ruin my future life by allowing myself to get caught up in being unhappy over something I can never change.

I'd rather focus now on the life I have ahead of me – friends, going to concerts, having fun at the beach, college, work, getting married one day and having my own children – rather than dwelling on what happened years ago.

I think my English Mum and I are both strong people but then neither of us has ever really had any other choice.

As both mother and daughter together, when it comes to strength, we're just awesome. To be honest I don't think there's much we couldn't do together if we just decided to.

The unbreakable bond, yes, that'll always be there.

So it doesn't really matter that now I've grown up, two voices, one story will start to become two voices, two stories.

I know we'll still always be there for each other.

Lightning Source UK Ltd.
Milton Keynes UK
UKOW06f1029140317
296579UK00012B/41/P